Teaching as Though Students Mattered

Joseph Katz, *Editor*

NEW DIRECTIONS FOR TEACHING AND LEARNING
KENNETH E. EBLE, *Editor-in-Chief*

Number 21, March 1985

Paperback sourcebooks in
The Jossey-Bass Higher Education Series

Jossey-Bass Inc., Publishers
San Francisco • Washington • London

Joseph Katz (Ed.).
Teaching as Though Students Mattered.
New Directions for Teaching and Learning, no. 21.
San Francisco: Jossey-Bass, 1985.

New Directions for Teaching and Learning Series
Kenneth E. Eble, *Editor-in-Chief*

New Directions for Teaching and Learning is published quarterly
by Jossey-Bass Inc., Publishers. Subscriptions, single-issue
orders, change of address notices, undelivered copies, and other
correspondence should be sent to Subscriptions, Jossey-Bass Inc.,
Publishers, 433 California Street, San Francisco, California 94104.

Editorial correspondence should be sent to the Editor-in-Chief,
Kenneth E. Eble, Department of English, University of Utah,
Salt Lake City, Utah 84112.

Library of Congress Catalogue Card Number LC 84-82380

International Standard Serial Number ISSN 0271-0633

International Standard Book Number ISBN 87589-771-1

Cover art by Willi Baum

Manufactured in the United States of America

Ordering Information

The paperback sourcebooks listed below are published quarterly and can be ordered either by subscription or single-copy.

Subscriptions cost $35.00 per year for institutions, agencies, and libraries. Individuals can subscribe at the special rate of $25.00 per year *if payment is by personal check.* (Note that the full rate of $35.00 applies if payment is by institutional check, even if the subscription is designated for an individual.) Standing orders are accepted. Subscriptions normally begin with the first of the four sourcebooks in the current publication year of the series. When ordering, please indicate if you prefer your subscription to begin with the first issue of the *coming* year.

Single copies are available at $8.95 when payment accompanies order, and *all single-copy orders under $25.00 must include payment.* (California, New Jersey, New York, and Washington, D.C., residents please include appropriate sales tax.) For billed orders, cost per copy is $8.95 plus postage and handling. (Prices subject to change without notice.)

Bulk orders (ten or more copies) of any individual sourcebook are available at the following discounted prices: 10–49 copies, $8.05 each; 50–100 copies, $7.15 each; over 100 copies, *inquire.* Sales tax and postage and handling charges apply as for single copy orders.

To ensure correct and prompt delivery, all orders must give either the *name of an individual* or an *official purchase order number.* Please submit your order as follows:

Subscriptions: specify series and year subscription is to begin.
Single Copies: specify sourcebook code (such as, TL8) and first two words of title.

Mail orders for United States and Possessions, Latin America, Canada, Japan, Australia, and New Zealand to:
Jossey-Bass Inc., Publishers
433 California Street
San Francisco, California 94104

Mail orders for all other parts of the world to:
Jossey-Bass Limited
28 Banner Street
London EC1Y 8QE

New Directions for Teaching and Learning Series
Kenneth E. Eble, *Editor-in-Chief*

Contents

Editor's Notes

Good teaching is informed by attention both to formal research and to daily practice. How students learn has been the subject of much formal inquiry. At the same time, it is a mystery that practicing teachers confront every day. The volumes in this *New Directions* series have tried to bring both — research into teaching and learning and practical experiences of teachers and learners — to the attention of a wide audience.

In the seventh volume of this series, Warren Bryan Martin assembled a group of chapters in which experienced teachers reflected on significant experiences through which they had learned or failed to learn. This volume is closely related to that one in that it consists of investigations by college teachers of how students learn and of how they might better be helped to learn. The authors assembled in 1978–1981 as participants in a Fund for the Improvement of Post-Secondary Education (FIPSE) project directed by Mildred Henry and Joseph Katz, the editor of this volume. They were encouraged to engage in their own investigations of the classroom using available theory wherever possible and seeking to apply and expand it in contact with the students before them. The authors represent a wide array of institutions and academic fields. They share a belief that faculty development efforts should become more particularlized; that is, methods should be adapted to differences in subject matter, student cognitive style and level of development, and the nature of specific courses. The contributors to this volume focus on different aspects of their classrooms, and they have tried many different methods to foster learning in their students. One thing ties them all together: their strong sense of the need for engaging in detailed observations of students if pedagogy is to become an art based on inquiry. In that spirit, the chapters that follow are to be read as samples of ways in which individual faculty have responded to the challenge of finding fresh ways of reaching their students.

Chapter One, by Joseph Katz, establishes the central idea of the book: It is useful to base teaching on systematic exploration of students, the ways in which they learn, and the difficulties they have in learning. The chapter also offers a way of observing teachers and stu-

Special acknowledgement is made to Mildred Henry, who was the co-director of the Fund for the Improvement of Post-Secondary Education (FIPSE) project out of which this sourcebook developed and a guiding force throughout. Gerriane Byrnes Schultheiss and Rosemarie Cusumano helped in the preparation of the manuscript.

1

dents in the classroom that is likely to provide more insight into student learning than casual classroom visits can. Katz shows why we need to recognize the individual learning characteristics of students, the power that resides in collaborative learning, and the necessity of giving students practice in the purposive use of ideas.

The chapters that follow focus on the student, although they range through a variety of subject matters, classroom situations, and learning aims. Chapter Two begins, logically, at the beginning—with the first meeting of the class and with the need for teacher and students to strike up acquaintances that foster learning. Chapters Three, Four, and Five take up the most basic kinds of learning: learning to deal with words and numbers. A teacher of writing stresses how much students can learn about writing from one another. A teacher of statistics emphasizes ways of reducing students' anxiety and of increasing their interest in what they often regard as a dull subject. The author of Chapter Five, Alvin White, furnished the title for this sourcebook by calling his own contribution "Teaching Mathematics as Though Students Mattered."

The next three chapters move outside specific subject matters. Chapter Six describes a freshman program aimed directly at learning how to learn. The author of Chapter Seven has a similar interest and sets forth a number of exercises for dealing with ideas across the curriculum. In Chapter Eight, a teacher advocates actual impersonation of great intellectual figures whom students otherwise meet only in books—a practice applicable to almost all subject matters.

The last three chapters deal with the fundamentals of student learning and development. Chapter Nine addresses what is often the student's most perplexing problem: How can I remember all this stuff? In Chapter Ten, a developmental psychologist reflects on research and theory regarding adolescent and adult development as it relates to college students' growth. In Chapter Eleven, a graduate teaching assistant describes the morass of confusion in which his own undergraduate English courses left him and how that experience now shapes his own teaching practices. To reach our students, Joseph Katz writes in a postscript, we must pay meticulous attention to students.

Kenneth E. Eble
Editor

Kenneth E. Eble is professor of English at the University of Utah and author of a number of well-received books on higher education and college teaching. The most recent, The Aims of College Teaching, *was published by Jossey-Bass in 1983.*

The student must become an object of study for the teacher and a participant in her or his own learning. Student initiative, individuation, collaboration, and purposive use of ideas are preconditions of effective learning.

Teaching Based on Knowledge of Students

Joseph Katz

During the 1960s, the notion of the student as an object of study gained currency. Several longitudinal studies of college students explored both the intellectual and the emotional components of the student's passage through the college years. Since 1970, there have been no intensive studies of students that followed students during the years while they were in college. The expense of such studies and the difficulty of enlisting researchers for them are only part of the explanation. As institutions faced continuing fiscal problems and as the job outlook for college students seemed to dim, interest waned in the more humanistic aspects of undergraduate education. Students themselves seemed to have taken part in this trend. As Astin's (Astin and others, 1983) annual freshman surveys indicate, there has been a huge decline in the percentage of students who enter college with the purpose of developing a meaningful philosophy of life—from 83 percent in 1967 to 44 percent in 1983.

Coincidental with the decline of interest in student development, there was a marked increase of interest in faculty development. The term *faculty development* began to have some currency about 1974, and a majority of colleges and universities have had or continue to have faculty development programs. Part of the interest in faculty development focuses on the teaching aspects of the faculty role. This interest probably

J. Katz (Ed.). *Teaching as Though Students Mattered.* New Directions for Teaching and Learning, no. 21. San Francisco: Jossey-Bass, March 1985.

has been stimulated by the growing diversification of student clienteles, the need to serve students who are more variegated ethnically, socially, and in aptitude than they were in the past. Another underlying factor is the alienation of students from academic learning. Students are as eager as ever to obtain good grades, but their enthusiasm for the kinds of inquiry in which faculty like to engage seems to have diminished, a trend furthered by the increasing specialization of faculty and by their growing emphasis on the kind of research that they learned in graduate school.

Faculty interest has centered on how to motivate students, and this has created some interest in improving our knowledge of student learning styles and stages of intellectual development. Luckily, we have the results of the longitudinal studies of the 1950s and 1960s to guide us. Perry's (1970) book has been particularly useful, because it provides a scheme for seeing how the classroom could help students to develop cognitive skills.

This volume is dedicated to the notion that it is possible to envisage college teaching as a progressive art. That is, teaching can be based on observations and experimentation. The results of inquiries into teaching and learning can be embodied in fresh classroom procedures that in turn can modify established concepts. If we adhere to this method, we may be able to achieve a theory of cognitive style, cognitive development, and college learning that will rival the sophistication we have acquired in other academic subject matter areas. The starting focus needs to be on the student and the classroom process as objects of study worthy of the meticulous attention that we bestow on everything else that we study in academia. This means eschewing the clichés of the born teacher and the notion that teaching is an incommunicable or unteachable art.

Observing Teachers in Action

How can we put the art of pedagogical inquiry on a solid footing? The experiences reflected in the chapters of this volume suggest the possibilities for further development of theory and practice. Enlisting the collaboration of faculty colleagues in the improvement of teaching is a step in the right direction. Although team teaching has had a certain vogue, we seem not to have thought systematically about the benefits of having a colleague share observations of our classrooms and students with us. Recent work by Mildred Henry and me (forthcoming) has shown that regular observations of one's classroom by a colleague and regular interviews of one's students can enhance the teacher's articulation of how his or her students respond to the materials of the course, the classroom process, and the teacher's intellectual style.

We associate two faculty members: the teacher of the course and an observer. We begin by administering the Omnibus Personality Inventory, a learning styles inventory, to faculty members and students in the course under observation. The learning styles inventory indicates the respondent's thinking style, its balance of analytic, reflective, intuitive, logical-deductive, esthetic, imaginative, synthesizing, and generalizing cognitive functioning. This initial experience is often very surprising and revelatory to faculty members. We have found that faculty are usually not clearly aware that they have a distinctive style, which is often rather circumscribed. They almost immediately come to see that some of their problems with students are caused by styles that conflict, by their lack of responsiveness to students whose manner of thinking differs from their own. After this first step, we engage teacher and class in a year of guided observations of student learning. The observer visits the teacher's classes on a regular basis, preferably at least once a week. Both the teacher and the observer regularly interview a small number of students from the class to ascertain students' learning styles, methods, and progress. The teacher and the observer meet regularly to develop and refine skills for articulating student learning behavior in and out of the classroom. They collect documents from their students, such as notes taken during class, and they scrutinize exams and essays with attention not only to content but also to the learning skills and cognitive schemes by which students approach course content. Periodic sessions in which class and teacher examine the methods and processes by which knowledge in the subject matter is acquired, including the epistemological underpinnings of the discipline, deepen their understanding of the ways in which they learn. Our experience supports recent theory that increased awareness of how one learns is a primary instrument in mastery of a subject matter. This is true for both students and teachers. At the end of each semester, observer and teacher fix the fresh knowledge that they have acquired about student learning in writing.

One of the outcomes of this procedure can be that student learning becomes much more active. Students move beyond recognizing the "correct" answer on a test and toward understanding the methods by which the ideas that they study were arrived at. Originality, reflectiveness, and critical thinking are enhanced. Students grasp, often for the first time, what investigativeness really means. They discover not only that they are capable of it, but they also gain a sense of the profound satisfaction of intellectual discovery. Teachers can become considerably less helpless in front of their classes when they know why things do and do not work with their students. Faculty also learn how to teach students whose learning styles greatly differ from their own and other students'. The method gives faculty the tools needed for continual improvement of their own teaching methods and their students' learning capacities. Our procedure becomes even more effective if a group of faculty assembles repeatedly to discuss its members' pedagogical endeavors.

Making the student an object of study and engaging the student's collaboration in his or her own learning are prime conditions for the development of the art of teaching. Repeated interviews with the same students to learn how they have been responding to the materials and the teaching of a course have led both the students and their faculty interviewers to a heightened awareness of how students study and learn, and they have elicited valuable suggestions of how teachers might better reach their students. The interviews yield fresh knowledge about such factors as concept formation, grasp of abstract theory, and the pace that optimizes learning. It is astonishing that, although the means for observing students and enlisting their participation are readily at hand, few teachers have made full use of them.

Obstacles to Student Learning

Explorations of the classroom by Mildred Henry and me suggest that there are three great obstacles to student learning: lack of individualization, lack of collaborativeness in learning, and lack of opportunity for applying ideas to situations in which the student has responsibility. Overarching these three obstacles is the passivity that still dominates student learning. In spite of all that has been written about student initiative and the limited pedagogical usefulness of passivity, teachers still tend to treat students as if they were vessels to be filled. Students themselves are not unaware of this, and in fact they are capable of quite sophisticated articulations of the learning process. This is how Kurt Overly, a sophomore at Harvey Mudd College, describes the distinction between passive and active learning in an essay he wrote for his teacher: "When one watches television, the mind often seems to become a receiving instrument rather than an instigator of thoughts. A student watching educational films and television documentaries or listening to a radio news broadcast often finds himself in this situation, which might be referred to as *passive learning*. The mind acts primarily as a storage bin for data collected through the eyes and ears. Reading books without pausing to contemplate or listening to lectures without being queried by the professor allows the mind to switch into this passive mode of operation."

Interestingly enough, Overly does not see this passive operation as necessarily negative. He calls it the "beginning of the learning process." One wonders whether this student too readily accepts the ideology of many teachers, who consider such filling of the mind a good beginning. Is it not that activity and receptivity need to go hand in hand?

Overly also describes active learning: "Active learning occurs when one cogitates, or poses and answers mental questions. For example, during a televised news broadcast, one might wonder whether the information presented was fact or opionion. During lectures, many students might switch from thinking passively to thinking actively by trying to determine the logical consistency of the lecture. Good students are quick to ask themselves about the implications of the lecture or film they are observing. They also compare the lecture to previous knowledge of the same material, looking for connections and seeking to formulate analogies with similar material. Note that this purely mental technique of posing questions, comparing, and contrasting involves abstraction. The student forces himself to discover the general principles underlying the data his mind receives."

In the next paragraph, Overly says that "a most significant aid to learning is physically speaking out and 'pushing the pencil.' Adding a physical element to purely mental reasoning increases learning. The purely mental aspect of thinking is fleeting. The mind quickly moves from one small chain of reasoning to another and another usually related but distinct succession of thoughts, much like the rapid focusing action of the eyes as they dart from one place to another. Verbalizing and writing take time. They force rapid thoughts into a higher degree of conformity, rather like staring. Writing, whether literary critiques or solving problems, exposes flaws in logical deductions that the rapidly shifting mental sorting of thoughts conceals. . . When one takes a tennis or skiing lesson, one does not spend the lesson time mentally thinking about how one should ski or hit the backhand." There is much sagacity in Overly's suggestion that thinking benefits from concrete physical accompaniments. Experience shows that students who have been silent in class discover when they do speak that they communicate their thoughts not only to others but very clearly to themselves; in fact, they articulate them more fully than they did before. Application of thoughts in action, including teaching, is a powerful way of giving concreteness to ideas.

It will not have escaped the reader that the sophomore whom I have just quoted is capable of sophisticated epistemological thinking. His essay is just one illustration of the forces for learning, and for learning how to learn, that we can unlock in our students. But, all teachers have had the experience of asking students to reflect on their learning and of receiving rather tepid responses. Even in innovative courses that experiment with fresh teaching styles, students sometimes meet the instructor's encouragement of their freedom with dutiful praise, as if freedom had become the new way of being obedient. Many students need practice to become able to articulate how they go about learning. Such practice is obtained not through objective evaluative questionnaires or even through one-shot, brief, open-ended responses. Repeated and continuing reflection on one's learning processes is necessary. Whoever wants to elicit students' implicit views about their learning must also conduct the inquiry in a mood of freedom; students must not regard it as a performance that is to be graded. In my own interviews about their classroom experiences with students whom I did not myself teach, I have been impressed, when reading the interview transcripts, by the cogency of their reflections, which sometimes compare with the professional literature and which at times surpass it in novelty, liveliness, and imagination.

Individuation. Lack of individuation, collaboration, and purposive use of ideas stand in the way of learning. I will conclude this chapter by saying something about each. Individuation begins by recognizing the individual differences in thinking style, affect, motivation, background, and aspirations among the students in one's class. These differences are often great, and there is a natural tendency to overlook or deny them, because recognizing them almost threatens to be paralyzing. A precondition for change is time spent obtaining a sophisticated sense of the cognitive, affective, and other differences among students. Interviewing students in some depth can be one potent means for achieving such knowledge. In smaller classes, it may then be quite feasible to respond to a student in ways that meet the specific cast of his or her mind. In larger classes, such individuation is, of course, not possible. But, lecturers who have a sense, based on inquiry, of the sort of individuals represented in their classes can address what they say to the range of their students' intellectual and other dispositions. (We all have had the experience of seeing a "good" lecturer address a group of people of whom he or she knows little and not only falling flat but also arousing hostility.) It is often also possible to break a large lecture class into small discussion groups and thus move toward individuation.

Knowledge of students' many different individual thinking patterns is a prerequisite for engaging each student's own distinctive learning potential. For instance, some professors with whom we have worked have redesigned their test and exam questions in ways that give students options to respond within the same knowledge area by picking questions that are commensurate with their developmental level. (For example, Perry [1979] contrasts dualistic with multiplistic levels.) Anonymity and impersonality are enemies of individuation in learning — though it must be recognized that some students want to escape the teacher's scrutiny; that is a challenge, not a pedagogically acceptable fact. In many classes, even in classes that are not very large, students are not addressed by name; this tells them that the intellectual transaction does not regard them as individuals, and it lowers their sense of intellectual and personal worth.

Out-of-class contacts can be very helpful in promoting individuality in learning. The Harvey Mudd sophomore whom I quoted earlier expresses it well: "The professor must have frequent office hours and encourage students to drop by to ask questions. Students desperately need the individual attention that office hours provide to overcome the inevitable mental block that occurs when perusing texts and confronting 'It is intuitively obvious that' or 'It is easily shown that' or several missing steps. Specific encouragement is required to overcome a student's feeling that he might be wasting his professor's valuable time."

Collaborative Learning. There is, of course, enough of the wrong kind of individualization in the classroom, the isolation of students from one another. Classrooms often resemble nothing as much as the movie theater, whose occupants all focus on the same screen in isolation from one another. Yet, experience and studies have shown the enormous power of collaborative learning. Scientific discoveries are often made by teams. Even the humanities, where writing and thinking are more individual, often flourish best through the stimulation of talk with peers, the vigorous exchange of ideas and perceptions. Here and there, teachers have used the group project method in order to make collaborative learning possible. One task for the future is to expand project learning, an instance of which is described in Chapter Three. The objection that there is no easy way to evaluate the individual's contribution to the group is absurd: Any teacher can find ways of assessing the individual's achievement.

Purposive Use of Ideas. The hardest thing to provide in the college setting is practice in purposive use of ideas. Yet, we know that the development of intellect and motivation requires the opportunity to use ideas. Teaching, the writing of books, not to speak of services and business enterprises, require audiences, people, and situations that one affects. Probably everyone who is now teaching has experienced that "learned" ideas become vivid only when one presents them to one's students. What would psychiatry or law or medicine be like if people were asked just to study textbooks without using ideas in courts, hospitals, and clinics? Yet, we ask students to learn concepts developed outside classrooms without providing the contexts that students need in order to grasp these concepts.

Here again, we can open new territory for pioneering. We will need to think of ways of making some application of ideas possible for our students. One though by no means uncontroversial way is to involve more undergraduates in the teaching of their peers. Further, we must think of expanding the sites in which students are offered an opportunity to test, apply, and develop ideas learned in the classroom to real situations; these sites should include our dormitories and campus environments. One crucial element is not just the grounding of ideas in experience but the opportunity for students to be at least in partial charge of a situation in which their ideas have utility. Ideas are then no longer passively received but become tools for thinking and action. (Of course, even a good interactive discussion constitutes use and development of ideas.) We should keep in mind that many of our students seek out opportunities on their own for using ideas. Students use radio and television stations, campus newspapers, campus businesses, and student government as opportunities for applying ideas. However, too often few connections are made between these enterprises and the classroom. This deprives the enterprises of the understanding and guidance that the classroom could provide, and it deprives the classroom of the vivifying impact of these experiences. Worse, the linkage between ideas and experience and action remains obscure, and the anti-intellectualism (or nonintellectualism) that we sometimes encounter among alumni may be rooted in the fact that ideas seem to remain the property of professors, not of students. Kant was right: Ideas without experience are sterile, and experience without concepts is blind.

The central idea of this sourcebook is that teaching should be based on systematic exploration of students and the learning process. If we take this idea seriously, we have much work cut out for us. But, the rewards are equally great. We can generate much new, exciting knowledge about students, the teaching and learning process, and the epistemologies of our disciplines. We can expect to see our relations with students enhanced by our sense that we are increasingly useful to them, thus reaping the pleasures of that often elusive goal of community of learning.

References

Astin, A., and others. *The American Freshman: National Norms for Fall 1983.* Los Angeles: Cooperative Institutional Research Program, 1983.

Henry, M., and Katz, J. *Turning Professors Into Teachers.* Jossey-Bass, in press.

Perry, W. G., Jr. *Forms of Intellectual and Ethical Development in the College Years.* New York: Holt, Rinehart and Winston, 1970.

Joseph Katz is professor of human development and director of research for human development and educational policy at the State University of New York, Stony Brook. In recent years, he has devoted particular attention to applying knowledge of student development to the classroom and to obtaining fresh knowledge of students from observations of their academic learning.

Beginning a class well means establishing a climate of trust that brings both students and teachers to collaborative learning.

The First Meeting of the Class

Stephen Scholl-Buckwald

There has always been suspicion between generations. But, there is also implicit in intergenerational relations a yearning for connection, interdependence, and collaboration. If we are to provide the best conditions for learning, we should establish a climate of trust in the classroom. Both teachers and students would like classes to start off well, but both experience classes that fail to establish an effective relationship between teacher and student or among the students themselves. The reasons are numerous, and I will single out several that, from the teacher's perspective, may explain some poor beginnings.

First, most of us received our training as teachers indirectly. We accepted the models of teaching behavior presented to us by our teachers, not as a result of systematic analysis of how students learn and develop. There do not need to be any recriminations about this fact, for those were the best models we had, and until recently there has been little helpful information for the college teacher about how to teach, about how students learn, and about how late adolescents and adults develop. Second, we are caught in our own life cycle dilemmas of learning how to be more mature, adequate, and empowered adults. We do not appreciate the larger perspective of our relationship with students in and out of class as part of our own changing being. Third, because

J. Katz (Ed.). *Teaching as Though Students Mattered.* New Directions for
Teaching and Learning, no. 21. San Francisco: Jossey-Bass, March 1985.

we are human, we usually approach the first day of class so concerned about our own performance and our own expectations for what is important that we seldom reflect on the student's needs and concerns. Fourth, we do not make sufficient use of our own personal histories in the search for understanding. We are committed seekers of truth, of competence in a discipline and in living, and of humane and fulfilling relationships. When we walk into the classroom, we too easily become authorities rather than seekers, and thus we foreclose the richest possibility for learning.

Teachers who consistently have difficulty beginning a class may not recognize these experiences and attitudes, which get in the way of establishing relationships. Students may not give them much help. Many have had years of schooling in mistrust and competition. They walk into class with expectations that are reasonable, given their experiences. Stanford Ericksen (1974) has pointed out that students enter every classroom on the first day with at least four questions: Is this class going to meet my needs? Is the teacher competent? Is he or she fair? Will he or she care about me? It is the last question that most closely parallels the hopes that we have for any new acquaintance.

First-Meeting Exercises

Establishing a climate of trust in which relationships beneficial to learning can flourish should be an overarching initial objective of any class. What follows are descriptions of a number of first-meeting exercises that work well both in dispensing necessary information and in giving practice for interaction within a class.

The Naming Circle. The simplest exercise is the naming circle, a game often used as an icebreaker for parties. A group gets into a circle, and the first person gives her name. The second person gives the name of the first person and his own name, and the third person gives the names of the first two people followed by her own name. The cycle continues until it returns to the first person. The teacher is part of the circle. The game may continue through the first several people a second time. Most people get stumped occasionally, but, as they listen to the names repeating and begin to find details—personal appearance, clothes, offhand remarks made during the process—that trigger their memory of the names, a group as large as two dozen can learn most of the names in a few minutes. The exercise usually produces a good deal of laughter and breaks the pattern of stuffy first-day roll calls. As in most of the other exercises, the teacher is included as another person rather than as someone apart from the class.

Introduce Your Neighbor. More interesting, more time-consuming, and more productive in terms of the knowledge that it provides is the familiar introduce your neighbor exercise. The class pairs off in twos, and each pair spends two to five minutes introducing themselves to each other. The students are usually asked to get together with someone whom they do not know well and to share a variety of details about themselves—where they were born, where they went to school, why they are taking the class, why they are majoring in a certain subject or pursuing a certain career goal, what they do in addition to going to school, what they already know about the subject matter, and so forth. At the end of the period, each person has a short time in which to introduce her partner to the class. The exercise provides a great deal of information quickly, it gives each individual a fair notion of at least one other person in the class, and it establishes a basis for future class interaction. It can also be the jumping-off point for a first lecture about why we study the subject, the variety of resources in the classroom—all these interesting people with such varied backgrounds—or some other topic. The exercise works with a group as large as two dozen, but the introductions become tedious as the group exceeds twenty. If time is limited or the group is large, introductions can be made within two or more subgroups.

Interviews. An expanded version of the first two exercises assigns students to interview each other outside class and come prepared for introductions at the next class meeting. If the teaching of writing (or language) is an integral part of the course, each student can be asked to write a short sketch of the partner. The learning process can be further extended by having the interviewee review the description before it is turned in so that the interviewer can do a second draft if necessary. One can easily see how such an assignment can incorporate a variety of instructional objectives while giving students rich information about their classmates. One can ask the class itself to set some objectives for the exercise or to list the kinds of things that its members would like to know about each other. The teacher should be one of the partners, too. Modeling a collaborative mode of learning is one organic goal of all such exercises.

Other Considerations for First Meetings of a Class

Gathering and Exchanging Information. Getting-acquainted exercises can also be used as a means of gathering information about students' knowledge of the subject matter, how they think, and why they are interested in the course. A written interest survey completed on the first day (or at home as a second-day assignment) can be read and analyzed by the instructor, who can make a report at the next class meeting. Oral responses in class can bring forth such information immediately. These procedures encourage students to probe their motivations for taking the course and to identify attitudes and background preparation relevant to the new learning. It is easy for people to give lazy answers, such as "I thought the course sounded interesting" or "It is required for my major." These are not dishonest or inaccurate or inappropriate responses, but they are not as helpful as more searching answers. We want to know why the class is interesting to a particular student and what characteristics of the teacher, subject matter, and other people in the class piqued the student's interest. These questions can be raised again in subsequent class sessions as students' knowledge of their own motivation and interests grows and changes.

Talking About Assumptions. One way of getting at the essential data needed for structuring subsequent class sessions is by talking about assumptions. A short quiz on elementary but essential insights into the subject matter can be given on the first day — not to be graded but to provide a list of issues to be clarified or subjects to be explored. Some commonly held myths about the truths in the field can be presented. Provocative insights or interpretations can be used to arouse student reactions. Students can form a preliminary assessment, do an experiment, or try to solve a problem that is prototypical for the field. If they do, they discover immediately what skills they need to acquire, what information they lack, and what resources they bring to the situation. They may even raise questions that they want you (or themselves) to answer. Central to this process of surveying student needs and interests is the objective of making the class student centered: No one should leave the first day of class without understanding how the class will serve his or her needs in some explicit ways.

Showing Enthusiasm. Studies of student evaluations of instructors consistently show that most students believe that most faculty are experts in their fields. Competence as a subject matter expert is largely a concern only of the subject matter experts themselves. Rarely do we need to impress students with our command of the material. What is not always clear to students is whether we are interested in the subject and whether we will be able to help them become as competent as we are. Showing enthusiasm for the field, skill in teaching, and personal attention to each student are major challenges for all instructors. Enthusiasm is not rare. It is normal for many teachers to lecture on past the classroom hour because the material is just too exciting to be constrained by the school bell. However, the faculty sometimes assume that the first point that needs to be made with a class is how painful learning is going to be. I have seen a mathematician go on at length about the difficulties that students will face in the weeks ahead and a language professor emphasize the discomforts that Americans can face while traveling in Germany. So, it is useful to ask, Am I exhibiting enthusiasm on the first day? Am I letting my feeling for the joys of learning this material show? One way to demonstrate enthusiasm and bring the student into the inner circle of searchers for truth is to talk about yourself and your own excitement about what you teach. A powerful technique for building students' confidence is to talk about how one has been excited by some topic, overcome some blockage, or discovered some essential truth.

The professor's personality, perspectives, and ways of learning will suit the needs of only some students. But, teaching can make most students comfortable and thereby establish conditions that will allow them to learn more effectively if teachers can share something about themselves that illuminates their values and styles and cuts through the stereotypes that students sometimes have of professors. Consider a tweedy Ph.D. who teaches statistics. The man appears to be bright, witty, perhaps cynical and elitist; he fancies the fine turn of phrase, invents ingenious ways of applying the statistician's analytical tools, and defends high academic standards. How do students react to such a teacher? They report that they are afraid of him, that they feel they will never be good enough to satisfy him, and that they will change majors rather than take statistics from him in order to graduate. We have all seen such teachers. He may be among our best friends. He can be great fun at a party or in committee meetings. Among colleagues who are just as keen as he is, he can increase the small pleasures to be found in academic repartee. However, we also know something else about such teachers. Most of them teach because they love the subject matter and because they enjoy helping students to master it. However, their first goal in the classroom is less to win favor with students than it is to find ways of helping them to achieve a new level of skill or insight. I once asked a teacher why he taught. His answer was disarmingly simple: "I want to see a student who comes into class afraid of mathematics go out feeling that she can do something with statistics." It is vital for such teachers to communicate this underlying commitment to helping students early in the term, before half the class drops out or decides to take the course on a credit/no credit basis, for the students' first impression is that such a professor is a hurdle, in some cases a hurdle so high that they will not risk going on with the course.

This professor might dispel a great deal of anxiety and improve students' disposition toward learning in the classroom by sharing something of his underlying philosophy of teaching at the beginning of the first class. He could tell students why he is teaching and how he intends to help them master new skills. He could find some way of identifying with students' fears of dimly understood and impossibly difficult learning. He could recount an anecdote about some quaking neophyte who became a powerful statistician in eleven short weeks or a mathematics professor despite years of long struggle. He could tell students that he knows about his reputation and how difficult it is to change the quirks in a colorful personality. He could even invite them to call him on his mannerisms. ("Professor Tweed — may I call you Bob? — I feel like I'm stupid when you say *Really?* in that tone of voice. Could you look a little less bemused and simply help me solve this problem one more time?") Finally, he could tell students about his own shortcomings and anxieties.

These suggestions are not intended to get faculty members to change major elements of personality but to lead them to make some useful adaptations in their teaching style. Sharing something of oneself with students will only clarify the possibilities for better learning relationships, inside the classroom and out. But, even if learning comes for some students in spite of who the professor is or what he does, it is best to declare who you are and why you do it early in a course. Time together is too precious to waste on games of interpersonal hide-and-seek.

Engaging Students in Content as Well as Process

Engagement between learners and teacher is not the only requisite on the first day of class. They gather in order to learn more about something, and at least part of the first day should be explicitly concerned with content. One traditional and effective approach is to give a short lecture or lead a discussion on a critical course in order to establish a justification for teaching the class and to stimulate students' interest in reading the material, doing assignments, or simply coming back for more. On some campuses, learning has become all too unusual on the first day. First days are filled with collecting class cards, establishing the roll, laying out the housekeeping details, and explaining the syllabus. Would it not be better to hand out a detailed syllabus, ask people to read it before the next class, and come prepared to ask questions or be asked questions about it? I am not suggesting a fifty-minute lecture. There is seldom a place for any formal didactic presentation that lasts longer than twenty or thirty minutes. What I am asking the instructor to do is to make a brief presentation of the core idea or ideas for the term or to pose a typical problem that will engage the students immediately. As another alternative the class can be divided into groups to solve a problem, provide reports on solutions, and then hear the professor describe ways in which others have solved the problem.

If a particular course has as a central goal engaging teacher and students in very personal terms with the subject matter and with each other, why depend only on the ordinary classroom to reach this goal? The most powerful organizational device for building identification with the group and extending information about each other is the retreat or extended group experience. A retreat need not actually take place on a mountain top far from campus, although an appropriate physical setting influences the outcome. At the minimum, a retreat can be a class period that lasts only two or three times longer than normal. Scheduling it on a weekend or in late afternoon and early evening may be sufficient. Including food, even if only light refreshments, enhances the establishment of family within class. Most registrars and department chairs will need a bit of convincing that such a significant change from the normal fifty-minute class period is possible or appropriate. Inviting them to participate may be a more powerful persuader than argument.

Clarifying Grading Procedures and Standards

It has become common for instructors to list the standards for grading in the syllabus of the course. Still, there is almost always room for further clarification, and grading standards often say little about evaluation. The first day may not be the appropriate time for pursuing grading and evaluating questions in great detail, but a few simple things can be done. The final examination question (or the range of issues or central topic to be examined) can be presented that day: "Here is the goal toward which we are all aiming; here is what you should know or be able to do by the time we have finished this term." Care should be taken to encourage those who are apprehensive about their ability to succeed in the course. If grading is based in part or in whole on improvement, students might be asked to share their own goals and suggest standards on which they might be judged. Grading by contract is one of the best methods of building joint responsibility for learning and evaluating. Further, the teacher could give the final test or assignment at the beginning of the term and spend the following weeks working to improve the answers. A full discussion about what is fair and what would be challenging without being threatening can be the subject for one or more class sessions. Simply stating that there will be a full discussion about evaluation at the next meeting or within a couple of weeks may be sufficient.

Confidence Building

There are many classes in which something more than a benevolent smile and a few declarations of intent are needed to establish that a teacher cares about each learner and that the learners care for one another. Such is the case with most of the classes that I teach for adults reentering higher education. Confidence-building exercises often grow directly out of the discipline being taught. For instance, in mathematics, science, and writing, students can be teamed to explain to each other how they solved a problem. Confronting a simple problem together, they can learn that problems are solvable, that they care for one another, and that it is okay to collaborate. In my adult orientation class, I also use a strength bombardment exercise on the first night. In one version, a student describes to another what he does best in some aspect of life, while the partner listens and jots down strengths that she hears implicitly and explicitly in the narrative. Then, the partner makes a gift of several gummed labels on which she has written the strength words. The person telling the narrative pastes these strength labels inside his notebook, where they will remind him of all his reasons to be confident as he proceeds with his work as a student. This is positive reinforcement, not behavior modification; students are in complete control of their own direction and impetus.

Establishing the Value of Learning

Now, what about truth? We know that truth is a difficult, evanescent thing because, in developmental terms, we have gone beyond the absolutist notion that there is a single truth. We have lived through the sophomoric position of believing that my truth competes with your truth. But, our students seldom have our complex perceptions of the world and of ideas. Bringing students into the many ways in which we apprehend reality remains our most challenging task as teachers. Our goal should be to get students to collaborate with us in our search for truth.

When I was a new teacher imagining the eyes of my graduate school mentors still on me, I felt it necessary to establish my credibility by laying out the awesome intellectual context of the course on the first day or two. The message that I gave to students was very clear: Professor Scholl is a profound and complex thinker, and students must be profound and complex thinkers, too. But, what any particular student carried away from that class was often neither profound nor complex. Rather, each retained a few facts or concepts or anecdotes or references that stuck because they were relevant in some deeply personal way. But, it was often not until weeks into the course or even after the final exam that the subject matter or the wrestling with new constructs became relevant in a way that could transform students' thinking and judging.

Ideally, I want this vital search for personally meaningful truth to begin on the first day. Then, students and I can search together as colearners. So, I abandoned my high-flown self-communing. Now, I turn to the students themselves. I talk about some things that excite and intrigue me, but I talk more about what may interest them. The exercises that I use for getting acquainted and to show that I care and will be fair serve not to demonstrate my knowledge but to suggest how the course may be relevant to each student. There is plenty of time after the first day to invite students to explore topics and experiment with new ways of thinking, to marshal evidence, and to form interpretations. Trust in me and in each other from the first day of class enhances the possibilities that they will be motivated to join fully in such an adventure. Their sense that I will support them in their search for truth, even while I challenge their present ways of thinking and bring more information and understanding within their reach, serves the same end.

Reference

Ericksen, S. *Motivation for Learning: A Guide for the Teacher of the Young Adult.* Ann Arbor: University of Michigan Press, 1974.

Stephen Scholl-Buckwald is dean of the School of Liberal and Professional Arts at John F. Kennedy University in Orinda, California. Prior to that he was a history teacher and later Dean of Educational Services at Ohio Wesleyan University. He has remained an active teacher.

Learning depends on open, mutual listening and discussing that can be achieved in writing classes by making writing a collaborative activity.

Learning to Write Through Mutual Coaching

Langdon Elsbree

From childhood on, we spend much of our time learning to ask others what they like and to pay attention to their opinions and perceptions. Discussing strategy in a huddle, serving on a committee for the spring prom or some other school project, exchanging views on recent films or books, sorting out tangled relationships with friends, relatives, or lovers — in these and dozens of other situations we find that we depend on others to deepen our understanding, to plan, to act. At our best, when our ego does not intrude or we do not feel threatened, we realize how vital the insights of others can be, how vividly alive we feel while interacting, in short, how much we enjoy collaborating. In such moments, even our disagreements can have positive meaning, because we discover we have come to know persons better and like them because they are different. The most satisfying kinds of cooperation are synergistic: They give us the feeling that the total effect of the group is greater than the sum of the group's individual members. Such moments are possible in writing, too, although our experience is often to the contrary. At its best, composition is a corporate activity involving fellow

J. Katz (Ed.). *Teaching as Though Students Mattered.* New Directions for
Teaching and Learning, no. 21. San Francisco: Jossey-Bass, March 1985.

readers, writers, and teachers. Sharing views, experiences, or research with others and submitting them for criticism, discussion, and modification are essential parts of the process of effective communication.

Writing as a Collaborative Activity

Except perhaps for a few deeply held views or unforgettable memories, most of us have to sift through our impressions, feelings, and thoughts and to mull over the data we have if the subject we are asked to speak or write about is at all complex. Moreover, if the circumstances allow, we count on others to help us focus; we count on others to add perceptions and details, to probe and test our initial conclusions, and to help us recall or notice what we might otherwise forget or ignore. Beginnings are almost always explorations. Any model of composition that stresses only the final draft is distorted because it denies our dependence on others. Poets and novelists almost always begin their careers by imitating other writers, trying out their styles, themes, plots. They discover their own idiom and material only through a complex process of trial and error and through increased self-knowledge. Scholars and teachers usually undergo a thorough and often a long initiation, a sometimes tedious but in any case necessary mastery of basic texts, before they discover their own deepest interests. Scriptwriters and free-lance journalists usually must master several conventional techniques and forms before they hit on the medium or subject at which they are best.

One Collaborative Technique. To foster collaboration in my composition classes, I divide the class into groups of four. Once these groups have been formed, I fix regular meeting times and allow between forty-five minutes and an hour for each session. If possible, the groups meet as soon as possible after a paper has been assigned. The first of the two collaborative techniques that I propose asks each person to read his or her rough draft aloud, slowly, clearly, and from beginning to end without a break. Usually, reading should take between five and seven minutes. When the reading has finished, the rest of the group spends about ten minutes discussing the ideas, the evidence, and the content of the paper. The group should not be concerned with matters of grammar or style unless they cause ambiguity or incoherence but with whatever aspects of the analysis or argument they find interesting, unpersuasive, or needing development. The essence of the technique is for the student to discover how he or she is being heard and understood by others. The presence of a real audience maximizes the feedback. At the least, the student may discover passages, arguments, or assumptions that need rethinking. At its most productive, this technique can open whole new ways of considering the subject or extending the analysis.

To achieve the greatest benefit, the instructor needs to give students some guidelines: Try to listen without arguing and without becoming defensive. It will be hard, but if you begin by rejecting what others say, you will cut off discussion and discovery before it has a chance to occur. Elbow (1973, p. 102) gives some excellent advice: "Listen to what they say *as though it were all true.* The way an owl eats a mouse. He takes it all in. He doesn't try to sort out the good parts from the bad." The same writer argues that we are both always right and always wrong. I construe this to mean that we are always right insofar as we know best what we wanted to say, but we are always wrong insofar as we claim to know what others hear and feel.

The point is to be open. The instructor needs to tell students that, when they think about the feedback they have received, they are not bound to accept all responses as equally valid, but every response should tell them something. Even the occasional silence, where everyone seems indifferent and no one has much to say, can imply that the paper needs complete redoing because it is too cautious, obvious, or impersonal to involve others. More likely, though, the topic will be picked up by the group, views will be exchanged, certain points and details will be argued about, and others will be admired or agreed with. If the paper has a central thesis or clear emphasis, the group will usually return to that thesis and treat it more fully after commenting on particular aspects of the essay. Far from meandering or wandering, most groups follow a predictable pattern: the pattern of the focused bull session. Therein lies its value: the free give-and-take of conversation on a topic of mutual interest.

Everyone needs a chance to read, since nothing hurts more than being left out. The suggested time limit of ten to fifteen minutes on discussion of each paper helps to ensure full participation and sets boundaries that can prevent long digressions. Listeners should always feel free to ask the reader to repeat short passages that seem confusing or unclear. Chances are that such passages puzzle others as well. If listeners find themselves uncertain about the paper as a whole, they can ask the reader to summarize the major theme or argument in a few sentences. Generally, it is a good idea for listeners to ask any questions they have before launching into discussion. If the reader is uncertain about the clarity, logic, or evidence of some section, he or she should take the opportunity to solicit the group's response.

What are the primary benefits to be gained from this technique? The first lies in the opportunity that it gives students to hear how their writing sounds in front of a live audience. It makes them notice wordy sentences, vague phrasing, and wandering thought in ways that silent skimming by eye is unlikely to do. Provided that the student reads the paper clearly and slowly, the student should also begin to feel the body language of his or her prose. All prose works kinesthetically. It has its own rhythmic, tonal, and physical effects. The first benefit of the technique is that it allows you to begin to hear yourself as others hear you.

Students should know that they can expect to be understood some of the time and misunderstood at other times. Both experiences are important. The complications of the human communication process were best summarized by the writer E. M. Forster (1954, p. 101) when he remarked, "How do I know what I think until I see what I say?" And, to see what one says, one must engage in dialogue, where others help one to see one's own words; in monologue, we can be blinded by our own words. Finally, students can reasonably hope that revision of papers submitted to the group will be focused rewriting. If they listen in good faith, even if some of the comments seem wrongheaded or irrelevant, they will be freer in choosing what to revise and how to revise it because they now have alternative views of the argument, evidence, and composition as a whole.

Another Collaborative Technique. The second collaborative technique that I will describe can be used as a supplement to the first, or it can replace it. This method of collaboration requires only two people, each with a legible rough draft in hand. Each person reads the other's paper, underlining or noting in the margin every word, phrase, or passage that strikes the reader as unclear, inexact, or ill chosen. Then, each student should talk over the reasons why he or she finds the wording vague, misleading, or awkward. For example, in a short paragraph from a student essay on communication, one reader underlined the italicized phrases, which are numbered for easy reference:

> The third factor in communication is the participant's skills, *which are primarily behavioral.*[1] Successful communication relies on the assumption that a person *will be attentive and accurately listen to what is being said.*[2] *The listener must have a desire to listen and an interest in the topic that is at hand.*[3] Other behavioral factors include the listener's concentration *ability,*[4] and his attention span *must be long enough so that effective communication is possible.*[5]

In talking with the author, the student reader gave these reasons for her criticisms:

1. Why not just say *participant's behavioral skills,* instead of *skills in communication, which are primarily behavioral?* The original is wordy and clumsy.

2. Why not say *Successful communication relies on the assumption of a person who listens attentively and accurately"?* Drop all the rest, because it's very general and adds nothing to the idea. Better still, why not simply write *Successful communication depends on the trust that a person will listen attentively and accurately?* *Trust* is more concrete than *assumption.*

3. I underlined the whole sentence because I don't think it adds anything to the paragraph. It only repeats the idea of the sentence before. Why not drop it?

4. Why say *concentration ability* instead of *concentration?* It sounds odd, and, besides, concentration is an ability.

5. Strike everything after *his attention span* because it seems unnecessary. It is obvious in this context that *attention span* means being able to listen long enough to take in what's being said and talk about it.

The revision that the student reader had in mind would have read as follows:

> The third factor in communication is the participant's behavioral skills. Successful communication depends on the trust that a person will listen attentively and accurately. Other behavioral factors include the listener's concentration and attention span.

The writer considered the other student's criticisms, made some changes of his own, and came up with the following final version, which in turn became part of another paragraph.

> The third factor in communication is the listener's behavior. Successful communication depends on the speaker's trust that others can pay attention and show their interest. It depends on listeners who have the skills of concentrating and listening accurately.

Not all paragraphs will be as extensively commented on or as fully revised as this example. I have chosen this specimen because it shows how a wordy, imprecise rough draft can be transformed by mutual effort into a simple and clear final copy.

A Final Comment

When first trying these techniques, some students hesitate to be candid about their judgments and criticisms of other students' rough drafts. They may not know each other very well, they want to be liked, and they argue that it is the teacher's job, not theirs, to tear the paper apart. A few students will even say that they would be betraying each other and unfaithful to some unspoken student code of honor whereby every person's words are his or her own and as good as the next person's. Such feelings are understandable, but they miss the spirit of the whole exercise, and they are founded on misconceptions. The students should think of their relationship as one of mutual coaching. Like scrimmages during the week, rehearsals for a play, or working math problems together, collaboration is aimed at improving their effectiveness in upcoming performances. Together, they are working on beginnings, preparations, possible combinations, not the final production or big test. Hence, they have the freedom to make changes, improvise, and even start over from scratch. They have the freedom of alternatives, because they have seen their work through another person's eyes.

Many books and articles now exist to give teachers guidance in using collaborative groups to teach writing. This annotated selection of sources that I have found useful may be helpful:

Bruffee, K. "The Brooklyn Plan: Attaining Intellectual Growth Through Peer Group Tutoring." *Liberal Education,* 1978, *64,* 447–469.
Describes ways to train and use student tutors in work with other students.

Elbow, P. *Writing Without Teachers.* New York: Oxford University Press, 1973.
A classic on the ways to set up writing groups, run them with maximum effectiveness, and encourage communication among members. Includes many examples and exercises.

Elbow, P. *Writing with Power.* New York: Oxford University Press, 1981.
Based on the same premises as *Writing Without Teachers,* with many new suggestions and exercises.

Freire, P. *Pedagogy of the Oppressed.* (M. B. Ramos, Trans.) New York: Seabury, 1968.

Contains useful reflections on the connections between political consciousness, literacy, and modes of authority that repress or encourage learning.

Griffin, C. W. (Ed.) *Teaching Writing in All Disciplines.* New Directions for Teaching and Learning, no. 12. San Francisco: Jossey-Bass, 1982.

Ten chapters with implications for peer teaching on writing across the curriculum; the most relevant is Elaine Maimon's chapter on collaborative learning techniques for small groups.

Hawkins, T. *Group Inquiry Techniques for Teaching Writing.* Urbana, Ill.: National Council of Teachers of English/ERIC, 1976.

Discusses ways of arranging small groups and procedures for working together.

Schultz, J. "Story Workshop: Writing from Start to Finish." In C. R. Cooper and L. Odell (Eds.). *Research on Composing.* Urbana, Ill.: National Council of Teachers of English, 1978.

Useful on reading aloud, listening, and pointing and similar matters for teachers interested in creative writing workshops.

Wolvin, A., and Coakley, C. *Listening.* Dubuque, Iowa: William C. Brown, 1982.

Helpful insights and exercises for teaching students how to listen to each other.

References

Elbow, P. *Writing Without Teachers.* New York: Oxford University Press, 1973.
Forster, E. M. *Aspects of the Novel.* New York: Harcourt Brace Jovanovich, 1954.

Langdon Elsbree is professor of English at Claremont McKenna College, coauthor of a college handbook, author of The Rituals of Life, Patterns in Narrative, *and numerous articles on literary subjects.*

The nature of mathematics makes it necessary for teachers of that subject to overcome student anxieties and difficulties in dealing with abstract reasoning.

Advice to a Colleague on Teaching Statistics

Bonnie Kelterborn

Recently, a former colleague who had only a few students sign up for his statistics section confided that when he first came to the college he was the star statistics teacher, the one whom all the students wanted to have. Now, that was no longer true. He said to me: "Now they want you." He said it quickly, seeming not to want an answer. If I had had the courage, I would have told him the evolutionary process that I went through in order to get to a point where I felt good about teaching elementary statistics to nonmajors and where I wanted to learn more about a subject that many mathematicians consider a bothersome stepchild.

Mathematicians used to describe themselves as either pure or applied. We pure mathematicians were unsullied by the real world and felt superior to those who dirtied their minds with applications. The distinction was typically made by graduate students and some professors in the better research institutions. When we left the protection of those rarefied environments to teach in other institutions, we came face to face with students who feared mathematics and who had a great intolerance for haughty theorists.

J. Katz (Ed.). *Teaching as Though Students Mattered.* New Directions for Teaching and Learning, no. 21. San Francisco: Jossey-Bass, March 1985.

Shaping a Course by Responding to Students' Reactions

The first time I taught statistics, I stuck to the book, practiced the formulas hoping to get the same answers that were in the back of the book, and tried to imagine what words I could use in class between the formulas and the examples. The students in the course were a fairly homogeneous group. Most were business or social science majors who were taking the course because it was required; they would be expected to use some of what they learned there in their empirical courses. For many students, this would be their first and last math course in college. Many had minimal mathematics in high school, and they were either afraid of or disliked the discipline. Arithmetically, all they needed to know was how to work with integers, decimals, and fractions, if they could conquer their fear in order to do simple reasoning and not be frightened by the formulas. Each time I taught the course, I knew more about helping them with their feelings and anxieties. But, my first time through the course, I was more concerned with learning the material myself. I remember leaving the class each day frustrated that, besides spewing out formula and solving problems, the prose and connections and reasons and applications eluded me. The text provided little help: The examples included Santa's helpers, gremlins, and toy ovens.

The students wanted to know how they could apply what I was trying to teach them; I wanted to do that and capture their interest. Having taught for six years before teaching that first statistics course, I had run into somewhat similar situations before—but always with material that I knew. At that stage, however, I was unable to provide significant applications. But, the second time I taught the course, the formulas looked somewhat familiar, the problems were somewhat easier to solve, and the connections—or the prose that I used in class—came a bit easier. I started to notice examples in magazines and newspapers that related to what we were doing in class that week. As I drove home or swam laps, my mind generated thoughts appropriate to the course: the size of an interval in which we would expect an individual of a certain height to fall, the relationship between the weather and the number of students who showed up for class. I began to introduce such observations into class discussions.

What was particularly helpful the third time I taught the course was that I remembered what we would be covering later. Thus, I was able to cut out articles on the average life of a Volvo or seize on a statistical denial that Vietnam veterans exposed to Agent Orange were no more likely than the general populace to contract cancers or genetic changes. We were using real issues as examples and dealing with statistics. The more times I taught that particular course, the more relaxed I became, and I could support the students better in their anxious reactions to seemingly frightening formulas, tense test-taking situations.

Specifically, I was able to support students by warning them in advance of possible rough spots and by giving them strategies to surmount most difficulties. In introducing new symbols or formulas, I stated that I realized that their appearance alone could trigger irritating somatic reactions. To minimize such difficulties, I learned to take time at the beginning of the course, going slowly even though much of the material at the end of the course was much more difficult. I found that such pacing seemed to decrease panic reaction dropouts from the course and that at the end of the course students were ready for the far more difficult material. In addition, when we had a particularly alien-appearing theorem or formula, we would build charts together and do the calculation work in class. I expected the students to have calculators and statistical tables at each class and requested each student to do all the calculator work. During tests, I always provided formulas for them. I suggested that each student keep a list of formulas separate from other notes, and I kept my own current list of formulas on the board.

Resisting Theory. One year, the imbalance in enrollment in my colleague's class and my own forced us to switch some of my students to his class. During the first three weeks, I allowed ten students to transfer back. This gave me an opportunity to ask them later to help me understand the differences between his teaching style and my own. If I had been more courageous or if he had been more able to ask, what would I have told my colleague about his teaching? I would have told him to not be so theoretical. For example, one day near the beginning of the course, we were doing means and standard deviations. The night before, I had read an article about television advertising firms that tested viewers for commercial recall and impact. Using imaginary numbers of responses, I used the material for statistical analysis with the class. I did not need the context, but many of the students needed it in order to understand the outcomes, and said that it helped to make the class more real to them. As we worked with the numbers, we drew our conclusions in terms of the success rate of commercials, not in purely numerical terms. Although telling the interesting story took time, it captured the students' attention and allowed us to use our numerical results to draw contextual conclusions. For example, the testing company called a hundred different homes during the time slot in which the commercial had appeared the previous day. Those who had watched television the day when the test commercial was run received a score of one if they remembered the commercial and recalled some of the information provided. The mean score in testing five such commercials was 30 (that is, thirty out of a hundred viewers of the commercial recalled enough to receive one point), and the standard deviation was 5. The testing company could then report to their client that, if its commercial score fell between 24.5 and 35.5, the commercial was about average for the viewing public; if the score fell between 19.5 and 24.5, the commercial did not do too well; and if the score fell between 14.5 and 19.5, it did badly indeed. Companies whose commercials fell between 35.5 and 40.5, 40.5 and 45.5, or 45.5 and 50.5 had potentially successful commercial advertising. It was fun for me to provoke the students' interest, and since the example came from my ordinary reading, it made no special demands on my time.

Going Slower. I would also have told my colleague to go slower. He and I covered the same material over one semester, but he was always ahead of me. I knew from experience that if I took things slower in the beginning, dealing with students' fears and allowing ideas to sink in, they would feel more confident when we got near the end of the book, and their successes would enable them to speed up. Students need the time to understand the basics, to sensitize themselves to the notations and language, and to play with the problems and ideas.

Observing Teaching and Learning Styles. What else would I tell my colleague? I have learned that teachers have different teaching, learning, and personality styles. What works for one does not necessarily work for another. My colleague's emotional style is different than mine. I interact with a class, watching for nonverbal cues such as frowning, moaning, and even more blatant signs of frustration, seizing an instantaneous occurrence, involving students in the process as much as possible each step of the way. While this style is consistent with my personality, I first learned it as a survival technique when I was teaching in high school. In contrast, my colleague is a straight lecturer. The students often complain that he talks above them. I have watched another colleague whose style is similar but who receives excellent ratings from students. The difference in student responses may arise in part from differences in the nature of the disciplines. In psychology, a student may more easily relate course content to his or her own life. Mathematics provides no such personal context.

Learning styles also differ. Some students are able to suspend their need for reality and can learn mathematics perfectly well when it is taught theoreticaly or abstractly. But, it has been my observation that even those students learn better when there are examples or pictures or something tangible. As studies have shown, the major portion of a student's thinking time in class is not spent on what the professor is saying. But, I found that using home pregnancy tests to illustrate Type I (rejecting a true null hypothesis, that is, the test is positive when the woman is not pregnant) and Type II errors (accepting a false null hypothesis, that is, the test is negative when the woman is pregnant) made students pay attention. Examples that had particular interest to students appeared to increase their active attention and participation in class. Such examples increased the time in class that students could spend learning, and students did their out-of-class work not by memorizing procedures emphasized in the textbook but rather by coming to understand the underlying principles.

Pictures were particularly useful in explaining standard deviations and the z and t tables and in illustrating probability exercises. In teaching standard deviation, I would initially resort to a bell-shaped curve, with which most students were quite familiar. I would give the curve context, such as IQ scores, population heights, reaction times, or hours slept. Then, using the empirical rule, I explained that approximately 68 percent of the scores fell within one standard deviation of the mean, approximately 95 percent of the scores fell within two standard deviations of the mean, and so forth. Then, we would play with questions about those parts of the population that fell two standard deviations above or below the mean. Always we would work with numbers on the bell-shaped curve. Thus, if the mean height of American females is five feet three inches and the standard deviation is four inches, we would expect 68 percent of American women to be between four feet ten-and-one-half inches and five feet seven-and-one-half inches and approximately 95 percent of American women to fall between four feet six-and-one-half inches and five feet eleven-and-one-half inches. Thus, only 2.5 percent would fall above five feet eleven-and-one-half inches. What are the implications of such numbers for clothing manufacturers or the American Association for Women Jockeys?

Some students need pictures that they themselves are unable to generate for almost all topics. For other students, verbal explanations suffice, but it may take a number of different approaches for them to understand. Often, the students themselves help. What teacher has not experienced a student's understanding another student's question that the teacher has not and providing either an answer or a rephrasing of the question that enables the teacher to understand and provide an answer? If a teacher works examples for the class, some students cannot generalize, insisting that another example, which is a variation of the others, is something that the teacher never covered. One typical strategy that I use is to begin a new topic with an explanation of how it fits into the concept that we are developing or of how it follows from previous work. Then, I move from one example to another, each somewhat more intricate, and finally reach an example for which we need much more attention to detail or manipulation or sophistication. But, again some students do not see this developmental process; they see only a number of loosely related examples. I give these students specific things to look for in a problem or specific rules to work with; for example, rules of working with algebraic exponentiation are particularly amenable to such a strategy. I do this for inductive reasons, giving them a variety of specific steps that can lead them toward the general principle that underlies the operations. However, to consistently give methods of operation for each variation of every topic or type of problem undermines my goal of having students understand the principles and processes of the subject for themselves. I find that I can never get some students to a stage where they can generalize comfortably.

Reducing Math Anxiety

Other students come to a course with fears that the teacher may or may not be willing or able to assuage. In math anxiety groups, I have learned a lot about students who have difficulty with mathematics. When we give them verbal puzzles to work with, they tend not to try. When we give them colored rods of varying lengths and tell them to play with them, they look at us. We tell them to play with the rods as a child plays with blocks; they make unenthusiastic attempts. They want to know specifically what we want them to do with the rods, and they are frustrated when we do not respond. Yet, one major road to success in mathematics is a willingness and ability to play with problems or ideas. I also learned from these students that they are frequently afraid to ask peers for help, and some would never go to a professor's office. Perhaps it is even harder to go to the office of a mathematician than it is to visit a psychology or English professor, who deal with things human. We seldom do. The more difficult cases must be dealt with outside class, preferably in programs set up specifically to treat math anxiety. In less difficult cases, encouragement, modeling strategies, and patience may suffice.

I tell my students a particularly memorable experience that I had as a graduate student. It occurred during my first semester in a subject that became my specialty. The professor, a renowned topologist, filled the board with definitions, theorems, and proofs without even looking at us or desiring our responses or questions. As I sat in back of the classroom, which was filled with approximately fifty classmates, I felt that this was the end for me. One day, I worked up the courage to ask the person next to me if he understood a particular theorem and proof. He quickly confided that he understood almost nothing in the course. Together, encouraged, we asked others who we were beginning to know how they were faring in the course. We quickly realized that we all were having problems. We formed a study group and eventually did well in the class. From that experience, I decided that I was seldom the only one who did not understand something, and, drawing on my courage, almost always asked the question, much to the relief of those around me. I encourage my students to be brave. I ask them to come to me during my office hours or elsewhere. Then, I try to reward them when they do.

People think that there are fewer good teachers of mathematics than there are of other subjects. If that is so, it may partly be due to the nature of the discipline. I have noticed among some teachers of mathematics a tendency to be pleased when they cannot be understood. Their students reward them mightily for such obfuscation by saying that they are so smart they cannot get down to the student's level. Teaching is a complex endeavor. Teaching mathematics may be even more difficult. I wish that I had had the courage to approach my colleague and offer help and request his insights. I wish he had asked me to sit down and talk. We had much to learn from each other. We still can learn from our students if only we have the courage to ask them and keep our eyes open.

Bonnie Kelterborn has taught mathematics and mathematics education on both the undergraduate and graduate levels for ten years. Currently she is a postdoctoral research fellow in biometry at the University of Minnesota.

Answers are not as important as questions, especially questions that probe the limits of our knowledge. The textbook is not our master but an object of our critical thinking. If the class is successful, then students will write or rewrite their own textbook.

Teaching Mathematics as Though Students Mattered

Alvin M. White

The first class of the semester opens with the staccato click of chalk on the board. No other sound is heard for several minutes. Finally, the professor speaks. This is one of five ways of starting a semester recorded by Kiyo Morimoto of the Harvard Bureau of Study Counsel (1974). What is the message of such an event? Is it that human relations are secondary and that the written record is primary? At my college, it is usual on the first day to give students detailed written instructions about examinations, punctual and tardy homework, the exact percentage that each activity contributes to the final grade, and other information that is reminiscent of a truth-in-lending notice. Learning is presented as entries in a bookkeeping ledger.

However, there are other goals. "In addition to thinking, the student should be provided with the education of feeling. He should not be led into the abject slavery of formal logic and rationality... What is essential in education is a receptiveness to intuitive extrapolations into the totality of nature and a communion with her" (Siu, 1957, pp. 96, 99). Siu (p. 87) tries to describe "other" knowledge: "Although real, it is as imprecise as an exhilarating spring day... It is not dispensed in measured doses. It is absorbed slowly and subconsciously into the moral

J. Katz (Ed.). *Teaching as Though Students Mattered.* New Directions for
Teaching and Learning, no. 21. San Francisco: Jossey-Bass, March 1985.

fiber and intimate intuition of the person over a long period of time."
The "other" knowledge can be taught only indirectly (p. 93): "The subject matter is merely the carrier wave, which conveys the modulated
nuances and insights of the 'other' knowledge to the subconscious mind
of the listener. . . Without extra courses or time [the teacher] can soak
the mentality of the apprentice with suggestiveness. He can develop in
the student an awareness of the ineffable sensing and feeling beyond
the formulas and equations."

Mathematics is no exception. Although formulas and equations
are the most obvious parts of the subject for the superficial observer,
mathematics shares an inner life with poetry, literature, and music.
The English mathematician G. H. Hardy (1967, p. 85) remarked
that what distinguishes significant from trivial mathematics is beauty:
"Beauty is the first test." Many students perceive a mathematics course
as a haphazard collection of definitions, theorems, and problems that
are beyond intuitive understanding. However, learning cannot occur
with such a perception. The game of chess cannot be understood only
by knowing the rules for moving each piece. Similarly, it is not satisfying to come to the end of a proof of an isolated mathematical theorem
knowing only that one made no error moving from one step to the next.
One wants a sense of the architecture of the structure that is being
created as well as of how it fits into the context, historically and philo-
sophically. Zubin Mehta was asked in a television interview of June
1982 whether he had a photographic memory that helped him to conduct a symphony orchestra without looking at the score. He said that
he would be "scared to death" if he had to depend on a photographic
memory. Instead, he understood and had a feeling for the inner structure of the work.

Meeting the Challenge

It is a challenge for the teacher and students to become aware of
and to attend to that "other" knowledge. It requires the teacher to find
convincing ways of carrying out such a program, and it requires the
students to participate in a spirit that transcends the traditional goals
of classroom learning. Such a program emphasizes questions over
answers. "The cutting edge of knowledge is not in the known but in the
unknown, not in knowing but in questioning. Facts, concepts, generali-
zations, and theories are dull instruments unless they are honed to a
sharp edge by persistent inquiry about the unknown" (Thompson,
1977, p. 109). My questions are not how to solve a problem or prove a
theorem but why the problem is solved as it is or what the meaning of a

theorem is, how it connects with other parts of the text, and why the author placed it where it is. Answers are not as important as questions, especially questions that probe the limits of our knowledge. The textbook is not our master but an object of our critical thinking. If the class is successful, then the students will write or rewrite their own textbook. Albert Einstein (Moore, 1969) felt that his imagination and curiosity were more important than his knowledge of certain facts. A goal is to strengthen imagination and questioning.

A Creative Experience

Almost all problems in a text are solvable because the author has contrived to match the questions with the tools and methods needed to answer them. On the basis of such experience, the uncritical reader may come to believe that every question has an answer. A creative exercise that gives students insight distorts a textbook problem until it is no longer solvable. Asking an unanswerable question that is not related to the original problem requires breaking away from the mindset of the text. Asking a question that is related to the original problem requires some understanding of the structure of the subject. Could a problem that can be solved in a rectangle still be solved in a triangle or an irregular shape? How would a change from two to three dimensions affect the solvability? What is the effect of changing some of the numerals? Could the problem have been solved with the tools provided in an earlier chapter? Could it have been solved in an earlier century? Could it be solved with less information? Is it possible to have too much information? The best distortions are those where the boundary between solvability and unsolvability is evident. Studying that boundary and its neighborhood takes the class to the heart of the subject.

My class is occasionally divided into two or three teams. Each team invents two problems related to the current topic. One problem should be interesting. The other should be impossible. The teams are then challenged to solve the others' problems. The discussions about the problems, the struggles to solve the impossible ones — or the discovery that they are not impossible — all contribute to that "other" knowledge. Sometimes prizes or special recognition are awarded for the best questions. Such exercises can make students participate actively in doing and creating mathematics as opposed to passively learning facts and formulas. Although the "other" knowledge cannot be defined precisely, it is related to enhanced intuition; it is the essence that transforms the novice into an expert. The expert has a sense of the kinds of questions that are appropriate to the subject and is aware of some interesting unanswered questions. The expert has developed judgment that is demonstrated when approaching a new problem or topic. Whitehead's remarks (1967b, p. 26) are relevant here:

> This is the aspect of university training in which theoretical interest and practical utility coincide. Whatever be the detail with which you cram your student, the chance of his meeting in afterlife exactly that detail is almost infinitesimal, and if he does meet it, he will probably have forgotten what you taught him about it. The really useful training yields a comprehension of a few general principles with a thorough grounding in the way they apply to a variety of concrete details. In subsequent practice the men will have forgotten your particular details, but they will remember by an unconscious common sense how to apply principles to immediate circumstances. Your learning is useless to you till you have lost your textbooks, burnt your lecture notes, and forgotten the minutiae which you learnt by heart for the examination. What in the way of detail you continually require will stick in your memory as obvious facts like the sun and moon, and what you casually require can be looked up in any work of reference. The function of a university is to enable you to shed details in favor of principles. When I speak of principles I am hardly even thinking of verbal formulations. A principle which has thoroughly soaked into you is rather a mental habit than a formal statement. It becomes the way the mind reacts to the appropriate stimulus in the form of illustrative circumstances. Nobody goes about with his knowledge clearly and consciously before him. Mental cultivation is nothing else than the satisfactory way in which the mind will function when it is poked up into activity.

Examples

Euclidean geometry was assumed to be a model of certainty. The postulates were considered to be self-evident and true. The fifth postulate—that for any given line, only one parallel line could be drawn through a point not on it—was considered special. It was thought that the fifth postulate could be deduced from the other postulates, and this quest occupied scholars for two hundred years. Lobachevsky is called the Copernicus of mathematics because he dared to ask What if the fifth postulate were not true? Others had considered that question too outrageous to be taken seriously. The working out of the consequences of the assumption that the fifth postulate is false led to a revolution — not only was a new, non-Euclidean mathematics created, but fundamental ideas about the nature of mathematics, knowledge, and truth were changed. Non-Euclidean geometry enabled Einstein to describe his relativistic world.

Many definitions and relations are valid and meaningful for whole numbers or positive integers. For example, the factorial function $n!$ means the product of all integers from one to n. If $n = 3$, $3! = 1 \cdot 2 \cdot 3 = 6$; if $n = 4$, $4! = 1 \cdot 2 \cdot 3 \cdot 4 = 24$. This is simple and natural for whole numbers. If, however, n is a fraction, such as ½ or ⅔, the formula and concept lose their original meaning. It is an interesting exercise to try to find a definition or meaning for the factorial function that will be consistent with the case when n is an integer and still have meaning when n is a fraction. This problem arose out of intellectual curiosity. There are many possible answers. Guided by esthetics and other qualitative ideas, the question was settled elegantly by L. Euler about a hundred years after it was first asked.

If mathematics is approached in a spirit of playfulness, there are many possibilities for invention. Symbolic formulas can be translated into ordinary language and vice versa. Symbolic formulas can be turned upside down. Parts of formulas or procedures can be omitted, and the class can be challenged to reconstruct them. Procedures, concepts, and ideas from earlier times can be compared with current ones. In what way are they similar or different? Is the germ of the current concept evident in the earlier one? The ideas and concepts of many disciplines were incorrect in their earliest stage. However, rather than being rejected, they became stimuli for a revised, more correct idea. Whitehead (1967a, p. 244) comments, "It is more important that a proposition be interesting than that it be true."

Overcoming Student Skepticism

As with any new idea, some resistance may be encountered. The emphasis on the unknown and the task given to students of inventing their own problems make the class different from others. Because the syllabus is crowded, instructors often assume that there is time only for a narrow focus on technical content. Actually, a narrow focus on technical content diminishes understanding. Technical content derives much meaning from context. In addition, the meaning of even precisely defined concepts and words depends on intuitive understanding that is socially acquired.

Several activities help to overcome student resistance. Lunch with the students becomes a chance for friendly conversation about personal interests as well as about class. Many students do not know their classmates. Friendly relations developed outside class stay with them in class and encourage mutual help. Each student was offered a chance to complete the Omnibus Personality Inventory (OPI), which was one of the topics discussed at lunch. The insight that there are different learning and teaching styles as well as different personalities is very helpful to learning and teaching. In the future, I shall bring the ideas about learning styles and personality types into the classroom rather than bring them up only at lunch. Self-knowledge allows students to gain perspective about their studies and why their perceptions may differ from those of other students. Learning becomes more humanized and therefore more meaningful. Interviewing students was another very useful activity. It gave the students an opportunity to consider questions about themselves and their interests that had not occurred to them before. The interviews related the particular course to their other studies, to their ambitions and hopes for the future, and to their OPI profiles. Several students remarked that every student should have the privilege of being interviewed; it gave them self-insight and indicated that others were interested in them. The interviews created a harmonious environment for learning. The sophomore course in linear algebra is considered one of the more difficult in the curriculum. However, the students who participated in the various activities that I have described here commented that the course was one of the easiest and most satisfying.

Learning Without Anxiety

My efforts to eliminate stress and anxiety from a class seem to produce another kind of anxiety. Students are skeptical that a class can be anxiety-free, and they fear that they cannot learn in an anxiety-free environment. The students' response surprised me, and I have been seeking ways to convince them that learning is indeed happening, that in fact they are learning more than they are aware of and more than they would learn with anxiety and stress.

One approach is to confide in the students, to share the objectives of the course and the approach with them. If there are free communication and a friendly environment, trust will develop that learning is occurring. A small part of the class time can be used to educate students about education and learning. As they gain confidence in asking questions and inventing problems, they gain confidence in the growth of their knowledge and their ability to measure it with intrinsic standards. The development of intrinsic standards of knowledge assures a student that learning has occurred. Exploring the meaning and possibility of intrinsic standards by class discussion contributes to their development and definition. Intrinsic standards can be related to the recognition of the structure of the subject or its relation to its context. The *Aha!* phenomenon is an instance of intrinsic knowledge.

Piaget says (1974, p. 20) that "to understand is to invent" and that "to understand is to discover, or reconstruct by rediscovery." The Physics Survey Committee of the National Research Council (1973, pp. 1152–1154) borrows an idea from linguistics, where productivity is measured by "the extraordinary output of new sentences [by men] out of their stock of words and syntax. It is this that makes human language such a remarkably revealing mirror and so potent a tool of the mind and spirit. The same test is most congenial for any real understanding of mathematics and science at every level. What can a student do with what he knows to make a 'new sentence'? Traditionally, what is tested is not the ability to make a new sentence but the ability to repeat a learned one, at best somewhat rephrased and at worst merely chosen from a set of alternatives, like the door-pecking of a pigeon." The test of making new sentences can be an ongoing activity of the class. Practice of the skill and thought process increases understanding and confidence in understanding. As Thompson (1977, p. 114) puts it: "The nature of intellectual ferment in a classroom designed to promote student inquiry is such that the instructor will always feel ambiguous about who is in charge. As a matter of fact, no one is in charge. If the end sought is the search rather than the found, it soon becomes apparent that no person can be in charge in the usual sense. What is really in charge is a way of behaving toward learning—an approach to a subject. Both the teacher and the taught are caught up in a mode of inquiry. The instructor becomes a guide to learning rather than the authority who dispenses questions and answers. The student becomes in large measure his own teacher because with the materials at hand he must search for meanings and in so doing raise questions appropriate to the relationship he wishes to investigate."

Two Rogerian Experiments

Two completely independently attempts to structure anxiety-free and student-centered courses achieved similar results. Reading *Freedom to Learn* (Rogers, 1969) inspired me to teach a student-centered course in the calculus of variations, a senior-level course in mathematics. The students met in my living room, lectured to each other on what they had learned, and discussed the subject in an informal and friendly spirit. I was there to guide them by questions and remarks. We met in my living room because I wanted to emphasize the difference from the usual class format and hoped that a different location and environment would be helpful. I described the course in a published article (White, 1974), and I received in response a publication by J. G. Mullen (1975) who had taught a course in thermodynamics at Purdue University under the inspiration of Rogers (1961). While I met my class in my living room, Mullen met his class in a classroom and laboratory. Although both groups of students had wide latitude to explore those pathways that were most appealing, my course was guided by several texts, which the students used for reference, while Mullen's course was built around a series of projects. By organizing the course around projects, Mullen (1975, p. 354) "hoped to reduce the sense of fragmentation in learning that many students have when they work through a large number of relatively easy but disconnected problems."

Our approaches had other similarities. Both classes were essentially anxiety-free. In both classes, the consensus was that, although the course had been very enjoyable and the students had learned a lot, more might have been learned if the course had used conventional lectures and a text. Mullen (1975, p. 359) writes, "I doubt that they would have learned more... although they might have suffered more... The approach not only increases the vitality of student questions but the range as well."

Two reasons why some students think that they did not learn as much as they would have in a conventional format is that their learning seemed not to be work but rather play or that learning occurred to satisfy a personal need rather than a teacher's demand. Both Rogerian experiments were guided by the teacher's vision of an educational situation that made the student the central figure. And, in both the teacher was transformed by the experience, because the teacher shared the students' learning and growth. The absence of anxiety also applies to the teacher, who can risk exploring new ideas and participate in the learning and growing process.

In my class, the students duplicated their notes, which were distributed to everyone. The final set of common notes totaled about 150 pages. It paralleled a conventional text in having a beginning, middle, and end. In addition, each student wrote an individual in-depth paper on a particular aspect of the subject. We started with no set syllabus and no prescribed text. We ended with a coherent course of study that ranged wider and deeper than a comparable conventional course. My motivation was to conduct a mathematics course with the same spirit of give-and-take, of intellectual excitement that I imagine an idealized seminar in Shakespeare to have. I believe that mathematics is not an exception among the liberal arts. My hope is to nurture creativity and to help students acquire confidence in their abilities.

The Paradox of Coverage

There is so much material that I had to rush to cover it all when I taught it in a straightforward way. Paradoxically, when I undertook to raise the cognitive level of questioning and broadened the students' and my concern with the conceptual development and structure of the subject, there was lots of time to cover the material. In fact, there now is usually extra time at the end of the semester. Since many of my colleagues consider it a minor miracle to cover a syllabus in a straightforward way, it does seem that there is a paradox here. How can we explain it? The explanation could lie in attitudes—of the students as well as of the teacher. The absence of anxiety, the sense of ownership in invented problems and questions, the recognition of structure and inherent beauty, the feeling of play rather than work—all may contribute to the success. Further explanations might be found in the apparently paraparadoxical ideas of Gallwey (1974), who discovered the importance of relaxed concentration and of not trying too hard. He relates the process of learning to play tennis to the process of learning to walk or talk. The process uses our unconscious mind more than it does the deliberate self-conscious mind. The process does not have to be learned. Indeed, we need to unlearn the habits that interfere with it and then just let it happen.

A conclusive explanation is not easy, but consideration of the values or value system of the classroom will illuminate the issues. If the students and teacher believe that facts and formulas are most important and then proceed to "cover" them in a linear, sequential manner, there is little opportunity for economy of effort. However, if concepts and meanings are embedded in philosophical and historical contexts, metaphors, images, and intuitions allow a broad sweep of understanding to carry the class along with excitement, élan, and economy.

References

Gallwey, W. T. *The Inner Game of Tennis.* New York: Random House, 1974.

Hardy, G. H. *A Mathematician's Apology.* Cambridge, England: Cambridge University Press, 1967. (Originally published 1940.)

Moore, A. D. *Invention, Discovery, and Creativity.* Garden City, N.Y.: Anchor Books, 1969.

Morimoto, K. "Five Openings." Transcript of audio tape. Cambridge, Mass.: Bureau of Study Counsel, 1974.

Mullen, J. G. "An Attempt at a Personalized Course in Thermodynamics." *American Journal of Physics,* 1975, *43* (4), 354–360.

Physics Survey Committee, National Research Council. *Physics in Perspective.* Vol. 2, Part B. Washington, D.C.: National Academy of Sciences, 1973.

Piaget, J. *To Understand Is to Invent.* (G. A. Roberts, Trans.) New York: Viking Press, 1974.

Rogers, C. R. *On Becoming a Person.* Boston: Houghton Mifflin, 1961.

Rogers, C. R. *Freedom to Learn.* Columbus, Ohio: Merrill, 1969.

Siu, R. G. H. *The Tao of Science.* Cambridge, Mass.: M.I.T. Press, 1957.

Thompson, R. "Learning to Question." In S. C. Scholl and S. E. Inglis (Eds.), *Teaching in Higher Education: Readings for Faculty.* Columbus: Ohio Board of Regents, 1977. (Originally published 1969.)

White, A. M. "Humanistic Mathematics: An Experiment." *Education,* 1974, *95* (2).

Whitehead, A. N. *Adventures of Ideas.* New York: Free Press, 1967a. (Originally published 1933.)

Whitehead, A. N. *The Aims of Education.* New York: Free Press, 1967b. (Originally published 1929.)

Alvin M. White is professor of mathematics at Harvey Mudd College of the Claremont Consortium. From 1977 to 1981, he was director of a FIPSE project on new interdisciplinary, holistic approaches to teaching and learning.

Cooperating faculty from a variety of disciplines can enhance the capacity of students to monitor their own learning how to learn.

A Freshman Program: Learning How to Learn

Larry Cobb, Clyde Combs, Ann Kemmerer

A new dynamic pervades classroom and campus as colleges lower the barriers to admission and recruit students previously deemed unqualified. The student population increasingly resembles a cross section of society at large. A small group of faculty at Slippery Rock University responded to the altered student population by developing a course that would advance the whole range of students — the bright, motivated, and gifted as well as those who entered college under a special admission program designed to overcome academic, social, and economic deficiencies. The faculty had two goals: to prepare students for a life of reflective thought, esthetic appreciation, and active participation in society and to convince colleagues that their frustration with shifting, even declining, classroom standards and their ebbing personal career satisfaction were not permanent.

Building a Learning Subculture

The resulting program is known as Human Inquiry. Its core is epistemology: learning how to learn in various academic disciplines and studying and reflecting on some of the dominant modes of thought

J. Katz (Ed.). *Teaching as Though Students Mattered.* New Directions for Teaching and Learning, no. 21. San Francisco: Jossey-Bass, March 1985.

and interpretation in Western civilization. Unlike most recent intellectual heritage courses, Human Inquiry not only emphasizes the intellectual, artistic, and physical achievements of human culture but also the how: how to create, how to define problems, how to appreciate, how to achieve, and how to learn from the past in order to create a desired future. The tone of course activities ranges from the ethereal and creative to the plodding and mundane, from dance, science research, and individual projects to remediation in reading, writing, speaking, and computing.

Students were involved in the planning and day-to-day activities of the course. When students sat down to the table with faculty, faculty usually took student perspectives into account. The interchanges generated fresh and increasingly comprehensive answers. The faculty shared problems about teaching and learning with the students. Students pushed beyond the often inert and dated materials in the texts and began to question the utility of knowledge bound within the narrow scope of faculty specialization. Many students were uneasy at first, and some were even angry with the transgressions of role boundaries. However, they became increasingly competent, confident, and aware of their own knowledge, experience, intuition, limits, and purposes. They responded with greater variety and depth to the intellectual challenges of the course, and there emerged a sense of delight in this personal and strange venture in learning and thinking. One student commented: "Professor A thinks one thing, B another, C a third—what are they really wanting us to learn? I am a product of twelve years of school that told us what the teacher wanted us to know."

To generate a sense of trust and belonging, initiation into the course included distinct rituals, language, and private meanings. For example the professors entered the auditorium in full academic regalia for one class, then explained some of the meanings and traditions of the colors and designs of the cap and gown. Several sessions began with the singing of "Gaudeamus igitur," the international student song. The reading materials carried the theme of students' initiative and responsibility for creating their own world. Films, such as "The Ascent of Man" series, "Flatland," "With These Hands," and "Controlling Interests," portrayed learning from a variety of disciplinary perspectives. The course used Bolles (1978), Brandwein (1971), Dunstan and Garlan (1970), Haskins (1957), Huxley (1962), McCain and Segal (1977), Peddiwell (1939), and Ruggiero (1984) as textbooks.

The faculty generated emotional commitments to studying in three distinct ways. With encouragement, students began to discover or create a setting for studying—the library, study lounges, empty classrooms, or friends' rooms — and they learned to become less sensitive to distraction, interruptions, noise, bothersome music, and intrusions by friends. In journals, students described their feelings about studying with other students. They were encouraged to attend cultural events with classmates and to model desired intellectual behavior on campus.

The faculty coerced a few students into studying by setting due dates for assignments in order to overcome nonsupportive moods that such students might feel. The threat of failure was a tool of last resort and used selectively to ensure minimal performance in the long process of nurturing freedom and self-expression for faculty and students. Even as an interim technique, most faculty felt uncomfortable with coercion. Guilt was assuaged through classroom discussions of why stultifying deadlines exist and why faculty may be uncomfortable and ambivalent about authoritarian means aimed at the liberation of mind and spirit.

Without being thoroughly rigorous, faculty explained Piaget, Kohlberg, and brain hemisphere dominance as heuristic metaphors for ways of knowing, experiencing, and creating the world. Faculty presented a plethora of thinking models with the expectation that different models would appeal to different students and that any structured awareness of thinking was better than none. While many students could think reasonably well, the leap into learning seemed to occur when students had a way of becoming aware of their particular patterns of thinking and of experiencing the world around them.

Like the child with a new hammer who pounds everything, students with reflective, analytic, or esthetic modes may try to use just one of these modes in all subject matter areas. One technique used by Human Inquiry faculty was, first, to explain the lesson so as to engage the esthetic or analytic or reflective students, then to use the student's self-awareness of that mode to encourage him or her to risk another way of learning. For instance, in one of our classes in chemistry, reagents were distributed to students to mix, observe, and encode by color, precipitate, and so on. Students organized the data to create some meaningful results in a chart or some other pattern. Some students preferred one approach, others another, but by discussing their preferences they often became willing to become competent in additional modes of treating experience. Students became increasingly aware of the mixture of intuition, observation, calculation, and active organization needed to generate data, create patterns, and solve problems. Like changes of state in physics, inaudible clicks seemed to occur, and individuals would shift their attention from the outside event to their internal modes of thinking and experiencing events.

Professors, too, had their preferred ways of perceiving and judging. They discussed their styles of learning with students so that students could see they shared with professors a tendency toward one intellectual mode and that both students and teachers could develop confidence and competence with alternative ways of understanding and explaining different realities. The effects of shared learning enhanced enthusiasm and morale as students and faculty saw that a tendency toward excellence in one learning mode is often accompanied by meliorable deficiencies in other modes. With 150 students and six professors, rarely was the brightest student less well informed than the least knowledgeable professor. Time after time, some students knew more about political topics, a dance routine, a mathematical relationship, a chemical process, or a period of history than some of the professors. This was often evident in the small class sessions, where each professor was alone with his or her class. "Teacher stumpers," thought questions, and bonus questions on tests demonstrated to faculty and students alike an amazing evenness among people in the understanding of human experience. To show the importance of imagination and of going outside the usual boundaries of a problem, students were asked trick questions, such as "Name four presidents not buried in American soil." Such questions enhanced our awareness of the benefits of shifting perspectives and of varying the amounts of intuition, imagination, and timing for problem solving.

But, more than technique was involved: Students saw professors thinking aloud, investigating, making mistakes, and overcoming shyness or embarrassment. As colleagues departed for class, one professor might distribute to the others novel problems to which they did not know the answers so that they could struggle aloud at the board in front of their class and thus reveal their actual practice in problem solving. Exposing the process as much as the answer was the pedagogical objective. The results were a dimming of blind respect for expertise and an enhancement of students' sense of their own capacity to learn from productive mistakes. Sophisticated theory was shared throughout the year. The Jungian theory of experiencing and understanding the world and its derivative, the Myers-Briggs test, gave students a way of understanding others' behavior and for becoming competent in "quadrants" (cognitive modes) other than their own. A. N. Whitehead's language of nexus, prehension, and occasion was used contextually, with students following and intuiting meaning, although the language rarely came back to faculty in discussion or essays.

Human Inquiry violated the expectations of many students about what learning meant. Much of their experience, even from other college classes, seemed to say that professors and textbooks were the authoritative source of answers, that students learned skills, facts, and applications. Student hostility was strongest around midterm of the first semester, in part because grades were often low on essay tests, since writing and organizing skills counted along with the content of answers. Problems required more than an answer; students had to show and explain how an answer had been reached.

But, students reacted very positively to the course. The celebration of learning was evident on those occasions when students applauded faculty presentations. Friends of students as well as members of faculty families often attended classes and field trips and contributed food, medical care, questions, and comments — all thus further shattering the staid, fifty-minute teaching-is-telling process.

Evaluation

From its very inception in 1977, the Human Inquiry program was controversial among faculty and administrators. The administration required formal research to determine the program's impact on retention in college, overall academic performance, and student attitudes and values. Although few regular academic programs are ever required to produce statistically significant results, the fact that this program had to meet such requirements provided it with an objective and legitimate basis for its experimental existence. We review that research here, in chronological order beginning with the 1978 pilot study.

The focus of the research was on changes in students. The Omnibus Personality Inventory (OPI), the Fundamental Interpersonal Relations Orientation–Behavior (FIRO–B) instrument, the Rokeach Values Inventory (VALUES), and the Student Development Task Inventory (SDTI-II) were used. Additional data were provided by Scholastic Aptitude Test (SAT) scores, the quality point average (QPA) at the end of the first semester, and student attrition. Four major hypotheses were tested. They concerned retention, attainment of OPI-implied goals, the meeting of students' interpersonal needs, and the changing of values.

Due to limitations on cost and time, the pilot study was limited to 405 students from the 1978 freshman class. The results presented here are based on forty-five students who took only the first-semester course, thirty-two students who completed the two-semester program, fifty students who volunteered for the program but were not admitted, and two hundred and sixty-eight students who acted as a control group. The retention data showed that during the year, twenty-four of the four hundred and five students tested withdrew from college. A comparison of their scores on the OPI with those of the students who remained in college led to this conclusion: The students who withdrew were better in reflective thinking, more interested in artistic matters and activities, more flexible in viewing and organizing phenomena, and more trusting and ethical with others. The Human Inquiry program did not retain students significantly better than other programs; the data also suggested that the university was losing some of its best students. Faculty members are still attempting to solve the moral issue of students transferring for what may be the right reasons. The programs, with the personalization, counseling, and individual attention to the student, may have encouraged students to leave, since they have clearer ideas of what they want to do and be.

In evaluating the changes as measured by the OPI, we found that the program significantly shifted the mean score on five values. Compared with the control group, students who completed both semesters of the Human Inquiry program improved in reflective thinking, developed more diverse interests in artistic matters and activities, developed a more experimental and flexible way of viewing and organizing phenomena, found a gerater appeal in ideas than in facts, and admitted to greater sensitivity and emotions. In the area of students' interpersonal needs, which was measured by FIRO-B, we found that two dimensions were affected: The program reduced students' need for being included in groups, and it reduced their need to be controlled. Only one of the thirty-six values measured by VALUES showed a significant change. In summary, the 1978 pilot study showed that the Human Inquiry had changed students' learning and personality characteristics in several ways and that it had met some of their interpersonal needs.

Students who transferred to other colleges, whether they were in the Human Inquiry program or not, seemed to be some of the stronger students. Although the retention rate for students in the Human Inquiry program was no higher than that of other students, we found that the students who had been tested for research purposes stayed in college longer than those who did not. A high need for affection provided the explanation that seemed to make the most sense. The testing seemed to meet that need, and it probably generated a Hawthorne effect.

As a result of the findings of the pilot study, the entire freshman class of more than 1,200 students was tested during summer 1979 with the same instruments. The students who were enrolled in the Human Inquiry program were tested with the OPI at the beginning and end of the program. Complete test data are available for seventy students.

While there was not a control group in 1979, the findings of the OPI were similar to those of the pilot study the year before. Means at the .05 level of significance increased significantly on the OPI scales of Thinking Introversion, Complexity, Autonomy, Social Extroversion, Impulse Expression, Personal Integration, and Altruism. The means decreased on Anxiety Level and Practical Outlook, the latter presumably as students came to appreciate the intrinsic value of thinking and acting. No significant change was found in the other OPI variables. The OPI data suggest that Human Inquiry students became more reflective; found greater meaning and enjoyment in intellectual, academic, and civic activities; developed more experimental, flexible, and imaginative ways of viewing and organizing phenomena; were more tolerant of ambiguity; and were fond of novel situations and ideas. Politically and socially, they seem to have become more liberal, non-authoritarian, and realistic; more interested in being with people and in seeking social activities; and less judgmental. They appear to have become less interested in the practical and applied side of activities and to value material possessions less.

Since a heterogeneous student clientele takes Human Inquiry, the question had been raised whether the program helped academically disadvantaged students. At Slippery Rock University, the University Enrichment Program (UEP) admits high-risk students. A random sample of students was enrolled in the Human Inquiry program. The data show that the beginning UEP students, compared with the regular admission students, were significantly lower on the SAT in both verbal and mathematical scores; lower on Social Extroversion; lower on Altruism; and lower in their development in Mature Intimate Relationships with Peers and Members of the Opposite Sex and Life-Style Planning. They were definitely lower in the amount of control they wanted others to exert over them. They ranked both Sense of Accomplishment and Imagination lower, they ranked Social Recognition higher, and they had a lower QPA at the end of the semester. When the students who completed the Human Inquiry program were separated into those who were in the UEP program and those who were not, it was found that the UEP students had changed in the same directions as the regular students. They remained lower in Altruism, but on other OPI variables they caught up with reglar Human Inquiry students. The program was beneficial to all who completed the course. Another type of review conducted at the end of each semester was a student evaluation of the course. The fall semester evaluation for the 1980 class revealed that students were pleased with most of the program, but students said that the two-hour lecture sessions were at times both long and boring. Suggestions for improving the course were numerous; the major student consensus was that there was a need for shorter lectures and more small-group activities.

Faculty Renewal

The results of our evaluations had an unexpected effect on faculty. The data led to extensive discussion, argument, perplexity, and speculation that resulted in revision term by term. In general, faculty renewal is a strong component of the program. Faculty development occurs on a variety of levels: through the sharing of faculty OPI profiles, through after-class discussions, and through peer and student evaluation of teaching. The team teaching approach, involving faculty from five different disciplines and as many schools, broadens the range of approaches to teaching and learning. The excitement and motivation of participating faculty are evident in the hours of time spent in planning and preparation, often with the support of spouses and children. Student-faculty interaction is extensive and personal in after-class activities, such as field trips, extra office hours, and personal, academic, and career advising. Valuable exchanges and communication occur on two levels: concrete action on specific problems or opportunities and discussion of how each faculty member exemplified his or her OPI profile and Myers-Briggs learning modes. The exchanges are often quiet and informative, but when they transform perspectives on personal philosophy, academic pedagogy, and general sense of what education is all about, they can be loud and intense. Many faculty, trained in narrow competences and specialized subject matters in the 1950s and 1960s, became concerned with learning in more comprehensive and varied ways. A striking early lesson was to recognize that the student's learning difficulties were often the faculty's as well. If the faculty had an advantage, it was in their possessing models and vocabulary that helped to explain what was happening. Even though faculty seemed to have much at risk, collegial support facilitated their learning in new fields so that intellectual risk taking proceeded from a relatively secure emotional and social base.

Small but significant changes are budding outside the boundaries of the Human Inquiry program. Students are beginning to assert their new learning-thinking selves in other classes and learning experiences. Attitudes are changing, as this student's comment about her new behavior shows: "I did miss something—I took notes, but I did not really listen. Now, I ask myself in other classes, What's the professor really saying? and I try to answer that." Institutional development is emerging as well. Faculty committees are beginning to ask for more information about their students, using data collected through the program. Some of the questions asked include, Do men or do women benefit more from the program? Does the program produce changes that persist over time? How do minority students' gains compare with others'? How do the OPI scales relate to the Myers-Briggs and other measures of learning modes? Are honors students appropriately challenged? At this point in the history of the program, a growing number of faculty agree that materials in each academic discipline introduce various modes of discovering, thinking, and creating; that the process of how students learn can be studied in each subject area; and that each student can be an active collaborator in the thinking, learning, and creating processes.

References

Bolles, R. N. *The Three Boxes of Life and How To Get Out of Them.* Berkeley, Calif.: Ten Speed Press, 1978.

Brandwein, F. P. *The Permanent Agenda of Man: The Humanities.* New York: Harcourt Brace Jovanovich, 1971.

Dunstan, M., and Garlan, P. W. *Worlds in the Making: Probes for Students of the Future.* Englewood Cliffs, N.Y.: Prentice-Hall, 1970.

Haskins, C. H. *The Rise of Universities.* Ithaca, N.Y.: Cornell University Press, 1957.

Huxley, A. *Island.* New York: Harper & Row, 1962.

McCain, G., and Segal, E. M. *The Game of Science.* Monterey, Calif.: Brooks/Cole, 1977.

Peddiwell, J. A. *The Saber-Tooth Curriculum.* New York: McGraw-Hill, 1939.

Ruggiero, V. R. *Beyond Feelings: A Guide To Critical Thinking.* Palo Alto, Calif.: Mayfield, 1984.

Larry Cobb, Clyde Combs, and Ann Kemmerer are part of an interdisciplinary team for a freshman year academic program at Slippery Rock University.

*College students can benefit from an explicit introduction to
ideas as ideas. Such an introduction can best be accomplished
by infusing an emphasis on ideas across the undergraduate
curriculum.*

Understanding Basic Ideas
Across the Curriculum

Sister Eileen Rice

In recent years, an increasing number of students have arrived on campus with inadequate preparation in many basic skills. In response, colleges have established remedial courses, instituted competency requirements for graduation, and crossed traditional disciplinary lines with programs like writing across the curriculum. However, besides attending to the basic skills, we need to examine the content of the academic disciplines if we are to address all the needs of these new students. In particular, we must recognize that the present generation of college students is ill prepared to grapple with ideas.

Professors, Students, and Ideas

Aside from the demographic shift in the college-bound population, there remains the fundamental issue of the different ways in which students and professors experience ideas. The students may only recently have attained what Piaget (Inhelder and Piaget, 1958) call the ability to perform formal operations, that is, the ability to think abstractly, to consider two opposing points of view simultaneously, and to manipulate

J. Katz (Ed.). *Teaching as Though Students Mattered.* New Directions for
Teaching and Learning, no. 21. San Francisco: Jossey-Bass, March 1985.

one variable while holding others constant. In contrast, the professors have been at home in this formal operational stage for so long that it becomes difficult for them to conceive of thinking in any other way.

Something can be done about this gap between the minds of students and instructors. Assumptions can be recognized and acknowledged, and explicit action can be taken to introduce learners to the study of ideas as ideas and the discovery of the fundamental and integrating role that ideas play in all areas of knowledge. Just as an emphasis on writing across the curriculum enhances not only learners' basic skills but also their understanding of the content and language of the college curriculum in general, the ideas-across-the-curriculum concept not only illuminates the basic foundation of each academic discipline but also reveals the power that these ideas have to integrate, clarify, and generate knowledge. The contemporary social structure makes it impossible for many students to connect with ideas as such before coming to college, and professors who take ideas for granted often fail to reach students who have not yet caught on to the fact that the key to much college learning is an ability to view the world through the lens of ideas.

It is critical to begin where students are, to proceed from a concrete to a formal consideration of ideas. The exercises described in this chapter presume such a progression both in content and in process. The content of the strategies, the material with which they are concerned, ranges from the stuff of everyday experience to the specific content of the discipline of the course in which the exercises are used. The processes used in the various exercises move, more or less hierarchically, along the lines of Bloom's (Bloom and others, 1956) taxonomy, beginning with comprehension and moving through analysis, synthesis, and application. Each and any of the exercises described here can be integrated into a traditional course at a variety of points.

Exercises in Ideas

Exercise One: Introduction to Ideas. The purpose of the first exercise is to provide students with an opportunity to look at one thing and see another as an initial attempt to look for ideas beneath the surface of daily life and to experience the diversity of responses to ideas. Both activities are essential to an understanding of the nature of ideas. The materials needed are file cards to which have been attached portions of copy from magazine advertisements; the copy is followed by irreverent questions, as the following examples show:

Magazine Copy	*Associated Irreverent Questions*
"If your passion is reading."	List five books you think everyone in the world should read with a passion.
"History repeats itself— beautifully"	Where? When? Why?
"Announcing one mighty number"	Which one is it? Why is it mighty?
"The artist as engineer."	How are artists and engineers similar?
"When you're turned out to pasture, will it still be green?"	How will you know when you've been turned out to pasture? How will you know if the pasture is green?
"The system has a warm heart"	Have you ever met a warmhearted system? Was the encounter a contradiction in terms?
"The energy we really need is already inside us."	What does this statement mean? Do you agree?
"100 events that shaped America"	Name as many of these events as you can.
Photo of a row of junked cars upended in the earth	What grows here?

You need at least one card per student. For convenience, the cards can be numbered. After each student has received a card, students take approximately two minutes to write a brief response to the question or questions on a separate sheet of paper, identifying their card by number. Then, the students exchange cards, and the process is repeated until each student has had an opportunity to respond to the questions on approximately ten cards. With a little ingenuity, you can find advertising copy that relates to the specific discipline of almost any course.

Exercise Two: The Word Idea in Everyday Life. The purpose of the second exercise is to enable students to experience the variety of ways in which the word *idea* is used in the media and everyday life. Each student is directed to ask individuals, preferably from a variety of backgrounds, to define *idea*. The student records the responses, and students compare the results in group discussion, looking for commonalities and categories within the definitions. Then, students collect advertisements, headlines, and news copy that include the word *idea*. Students are then asked to infer definitions of *idea* from the material gathered. After all definitions have been collated and categorized, students are asked to consult a dictionary for its definitions of *idea* and to relate them to the results of their own efforts. This exercise could be profitably followed by the definition of *idea* as the word is used in the discipline that the course concerns.

Exercise Three: Ideas on Ideas. In the third exercise, students are exposed to proverbs and maxims that include the word *idea* in order to develop a sense of the role and potency of ideas in human history and daily life. That is the role of proverbs: They transmit culture and moral education. Statements about ideas culled from *Bartlett's Book of Familiar Quotations* and similar sources are distributed to students. Students read the list individually and select the statement that most firmly captures their mind. Then, they reflect on the meaning of the statement, both its denotation and its connotation. To share the results of this reflection, the students form pairs or trios. Here they share the proverb they selected, its meaning for them, and their assessment of its power.

This approach to proverbs can be extended by having students check books of quotations for entries under the various Great Ideas, such as Animal, Cause, Change, Hypothesis, Law, Matter, Principle, Symbol, Soul, and State. (See also Exercise Seven.) The instructor can ask students to select from the list of Great Ideas those that are pertinent to the discipline. This approach gives students an additional insight into how the ideas on which the discipline is founded are communicated to average people by proverbs.

Exercise Four: Detecting Ideas in Academic Disciplines. To extend their investigation of the fundamental ideas animating and underlying a particular academic discipline, students will find that interviews with college faculty, graduate students, and departmental majors constitute a very meaningful activity. Students interview their informants for at least fifteen minutes to consider such questions as these: What is your definition of an idea? In your opinion, what are the three to five major ideas in the field? When did you first meet these ideas? What idea in the field most excites you? After all the interviews have been completed, a class session can be spent considering the results. Students with different academic majors can be grouped together and asked to look for common ideas that cross disciplines. This exercise in interdisciplinarity may help to dissipate some of the isolation caused by overspecialization.

Exercise Five: Idea People. Students evaluate world figures whose ideas have significantly influenced others. The list could consist of individuals in a variety of fields, or it could be limited to a specific discipline if that better suited the purposes of the course. Once a list has been established, students brainstorm on the ideas animating each individual and do further research on specific individuals. Resources for such research can include interviews with other faculty as well as the traditional print materials. When students report on their efforts, care should be taken to focus the discussions on ideas. Consideration can be given to such matters as personal and social factors that may have influenced the individual's ideas and ideas that individuals have held in common.

Exercise Six: Journal Sharing. A course bibliography is distributed. Students are instructed to select one book from the list each week or at some other appropriate interval and to record in a journal at least three ideas from the book chosen, together with a personal comment on each. In a periodic group session, students exchange journals and comment in writing on the ideas that others have chosen. Comments can include positive and negative reactions to the idea itself, related personal experiences, associated readings, and so forth. Generally, each student can profitably read and comment on the journals of three to five other students at one session. This exercise allows students to experience one another as generators of ideas, and it introduces them to books and authors whom they otherwise might not have encountered.

Exercise Seven: The Great Ideas. Having been exposed to ideas in a wide variety of naturalistic and somewhat informal settings, students may now be ready for a more rigorous treatment of ideas, and the Great Ideas (Adler, 1955) from the University of Chicago's Great Books series are an excellent vehicle for such analysis. The 102 Great Ideas are especially amenable to the analysis entitled "How to Recognize an Idea When You Meet It" described as follows:

> When you suspect that what you have before you is an idea, make its acquaintance in the following manner. Explain the idea to yourself as you now understand it, as clearly and briefly as possible, and then explain the idea to someone else and then have them tell you what they heard you say. Was it what you meant? If not, try saying it another way. Having gotten the suspected idea out in the open, check it for telltale characteristics of an idea. *Edges and boundaries:* For instance, can you categorize the idea? Is it basically concerned with something physical? psychological? sociological? philosophical? Does the idea refer to something concrete or something abstract? Is there

any symbolism with the idea? *Consistency:* For instance, what are the components and aspects of this idea? How do the various aspects of the idea relate to each other? Does the relationship allow the different components of the idea to retain their integrity? Has the idea changed through the years? Have these changes damaged its integrity? *Consequences:* For instance, how would the world be different today if this idea were taken seriously? How would the world be different if this idea did not exist? Would your life be different if this idea did not exist? Would history have to be rewritten if this idea had been taken seriously in the past? Does this idea change the location of power in individuals and institutions? Would different people be powerful if this idea were taken seriously?

If what you are considering as a candidate for an idea has fared well through these questions, if your potential idea has edges and boundaries, if it holds up well, and if it has consequences, then chances are good that it is valid. You may be the proud owner of a brand new idea! If so, cherish it carefully and make room for it in your mind. Leave some room on either side of it too — chances are that other ideas will soon take up residence there.

Each student selects one of the Great Ideas. Students have fifteen to twenty minutes to consider the questions just enumerated with respect to the Great Idea that they have chosen. Then, they share their responses with other students in groups of four or five; members of the group offer contributions to each report. Finally, discussion in the total group of how different students answered the questions with respect to the same idea provides some closure for the process.

Exercise Eight: Vertical Synthesis of Ideas. To continue the examination of Great Ideas, students can investigate how ideas are modified by other ideas over time and how ideas converse with one another through time. Such conversations can be labeled *vertical communications.* They are exemplified by Thomas's (1974) notion that composers of music converse through their influence on one another's work. Ideas are synthesized vertically when an idea from one period is modified by other ideas over the passage of time. In this sense, to synthesize means to allow an idea to be affected by other ideas over time. The summaries of the history of each of the Great Ideas found in Volumes 2 and 3 of the Great Books series (Adler, 1955) describe this type of vertical synthesis, chronicling as they do how each idea has changed and been modified by other ideas over the years.

Students can experience the interaction of some contemporary minds and ideas through The Great Ideas Today (Adler and Hutchins, 1961-) yearbooks of the Great Books series. As a rule, each volume is divided into four sections: an issue-oriented debate or symposium, contemporary aspects of a great idea, the year's developments in the arts and sciences, and additions to the Great Books library. The fourth section demonstrates to students that the term *Great Books* does not refer to a static body of literature. This is particularly critical for students who tend to conceive of the past as unchanging and unrelated to their own lives.

Exercise Nine: Horizontal Synthesis of Ideas. To apply the activities of ideas to one's own life helps to cement the bond between the theoretical and the practical implied in discussions of the contemporary aspects of Great Ideas. This activity involves the combining of two or more current ideas to make a new whole, for example, Ray Bradbury's (1957) notion of old people as time machines, Murray Melbin's (1978) research on night as frontier, and Maxine Greene's (1978) treatment of teacher as stranger. In each instance, a new whole is made out of two or more previously unconnected parts. Most disciplines offer many opportunities for such synthesis. English instructors may want to consider the poet or literature. History classes could explore the historian or culture, and teacher education courses could examine the teacher or the school. To explore the synthesis, students look up both aspects of the comparison in the dictionary and look for similarities between them. Then, they are directed to the same comparison in the literature, if it is available, and they are asked to comment on whether the author's synthesis differed significantly from their own.

Exercise Ten: Ideas That Change the World. An appropriate culminating activity for the concept of ideas across the curriculum from a practical perspective is understanding of their consequences. Such understanding can be facilitated by asking students to come up with one or more ideas that would change the world (or the humanities, or science, or history, or poetry, or education, or something else). Then, they take the first step to make the idea happen: write a letter, call a conference, send a telegram, publish an article, and so forth.

In a class in which I used many of these exercises, this tenth activity has had some astonishing consequences. Students have taken on corporate giants and national politicians as well as individuals and agencies significant only in their own personal worlds. These efforts have been very interesting, in that students are not certain at the beginning whether their ideas really can change the world. A case in point was the student who was disgusted because her children's lunch boxes kept coming unlatched as they walked to school. She wrote to the manufacturer, who sent new lunch boxes, which promptly fell heir to the same malady. However, her frustration was exceeded by her concern that this idea—things ought to work—was not of world-changing caliber. The ensuing conversation made it clear just how world-changing their idea was: The discussion ranged from quality of workmanship, to planned obsolescence, to the economic consequences of not needing replacements in a society plagued by high unemployment. If any one of these ideas were followed to its logical consequence, it would definitely have an impact on the world. On a larger scale, another student took one of the major auto makers to task for having fired striking workers in a plant abroad. After mountains of correspondence, the first letter in which arrived at corporate headquarters during the week when the company's international board of directors was meeting, the workers were offered the option of getting their jobs back or taking substantial severance pay. Mathematics classes could have similarly significant ideas with regard to the use of numbers in our lives, and history classes would have little difficulty generating ideas regarding the uses of the past in the present and the future.

Miscellaneous Exercises. In addition to the exercises just described, I have had students analyze Bronowski's "The Ascent of Man" film on Galileo ("The Starry Messenger") for the insights that it provides on the relationship between ideas and individuals and institutions. The film "Why Man Creates," with its memorable answer to the question, Where do ideas come from? ("from looking at one thing and seeing something else") is used in conjunction with discussions on the generation of ideas. Finally, I have used specific articles from the *Journal of the History of Ideas.*

Methodological Principles of the
Ideas-Across-the-Curriculum Concept

Like all curricular strategies, the ideas-across-the-curriculum concept is based on principles. First, learning is not a spectator sport. Students must talk with one another, both to test the precision and lucidity of their own intellectual formulation and to take responsibility for the learning process on the part of all concerned. Learning does not happen to someone. It is something that one does.

Second, learning begins with the learner. The process proceeds from the affective—where students are and what they are feeling—to the cognitive—what students are thinking about and how they can be challenged to higher-order thinking—to application of their thought to behavior. The assumption that students think as professors do has to be rejected on a practical as well as a theoretical level. Thus, a focus on the abstract ideas animating a discipline should be preceded by an experiential or concrete introduction to the ideas, and it should be followed by an opportunity to apply them to one's personal and professional life.

Third, both to facilitate this mobility and to enhance the attraction of the world of ideas, the instructor must reveal his or her own fascination with ideas. The experience of meeting and observing and knowing an individual who is honestly moved by the power of ideas in his or her life and who obviously relishes the opportunity to interact with ideas is impressive to students. The eloquence of such personal testimony is not easy to refute. Fourth, students must make connections between ideas and their own personal and professional lives. While modeling is important, it is vital for the connections not to be made on behalf of students but for students to be challenged to make the connections for themselves. That is why the exercises just described focus on student activity. Students do the analysis and synthesis rather than watch it be done. Activity is missing from many college classes, which may be part of the reason why students show little enthusiasm for many college courses. Fifth, one way of nurturing this activity between ideas and the minds of students is by giving them opportunities to own ideas. A variety of instructional strategies can be used to accomplish this goal. For example, you can ask students to explain the same idea to several different classmates; this provides an interesting way of having them report back on assignments that they have done. They will notice the increasing confidence with which they articulate the material. At the other end, you can ask students to generate some ideas on their own and to defend them before a group of their peers. The process of investing oneself in one's ideas is critical. The merger of theory with human commitment is the goal.

Conclusion

My thesis has been that college students can benefit from an explicit introduction to ideas as ideas. Students are often left on their own to discover the importance of grappling with ideas. The focus of all the ideas-across-the-curriculum exercises and the very rationale for emphasizing ideas across the curriculum is the challenging of assumptions: The concept begins by challenging the assumption that students think as professors do. Then, it helps students to challenge the assumptions on which they have built their intellectual lives: that ideas have little practical utility and that the ideas that concern the various disciplines have little in common. Infusing ideas across the typical undergraduate curriculum powerfully confronts the fragmentation that characterizes the experience of many college students in their coursework. The emphasis of ideas across the curriculum on a personal commitment to ideas also helps students to fill the gap that many experience between the content of their classes and the content of their lives.

References

Adler, M. *The Great Ideas*. Chicago: University of Chicago Press, 1955.

Adler, M., and Hutchins, R. *The Great Ideas Today*. Chicago: Encyclopedia Britannica, 1961–.

Bartlett, J. *Familiar Quotations*. Boston: Little, Brown, 1980 (rev. ed.).

Bloom, B., and others. *Taxonomy of Educational Objectives Handbook I: Cognitive Domain*. New York: McKay, 1956.

Bradbury, R. *Dandelion Wine*. New York: Bantam Books, 1957.

Bronowski, J. "The Ascent of Man." (Available from Time-Life Distribution Center, P.O. Box 644, Paramus, N.J. 07652.)

Greene, M. *Teacher as Stranger*. Belmont, Calif.: Wadsworth, 1978.

Inhelder, B., and Piaget, J. *The Growth of Logical Thinking from Childhood to Adolescence*. New York: Basic Books, 1958.

Kaiser Aluminum. "Why Man Creates." (Available from Pyramid Films, Box 1048, Santa Monica, Calif. 90406.)

Melbin, M. "Night as Frontier." *American Sociological Review,* 1978, *43,* 3–22.

Thomas, L. *The Lifes of a Cell*. New York: Viking Press, 1974.

Sister Eileen Rice is assistant professor of education and chair of the Communication Arts and Education Division at Siena Heights College.

*Reconstructing the classroom as theater gives both students
and faculty a chance to see thought brought to life and to give
the imaginative dimension parity with the intellectual.*

The Classroom as Theater

Sidney Homan

I tried an experiment of using the principles of the drama in the college
classroom with two seminars and a large-enrollment course during the
1979–1980 academic year. My source was the public television show
"Meeting of the Minds," whose host, the comedian Steve Allen, staged
dinner table conversations with five or six actors impersonating famous
historical figures, thinkers, or literary characters. A typical grouping
might include Martin Luther, Thomas Aquinas, Machiavelli, Florence
Nightingale, and Karl Marx, and the drama would be generated by the
interplay among these characters, who speak about historical or contemporary issues from an individual perspective.

   In the fall quarter, I used this format with a seminar of ten
honors students, all bright seniors. I invited five colleagues to come to
the seminar and impersonate someone on whom they had spent a
career of scholarly research and teaching. Our topic that quarter was
the concept of evil and the Holocaust, and our guests included Rous-
seau, Kafka, Hannah Arendt, Thomas Aquinas, Job, and Shakespeare's Iago. At the first meeting of each week, the students and I
prepared for our guest, reading major texts and researching individual
topics concerned with his or her life and writings. On Wednesday, that
guest appeared. There was one ground rule: We addressed the faculty
member not by his or her real name but by the character's name. The

J. Katz (Ed.). *Teaching as Though Students Mattered.* New Directions for
Teaching and Learning, no. 21. San Francisco: Jossey-Bass, March 1985.

gamut of impersonations stretched from the minimal (Arendt, played by a male colleague, came in without costume or make-up, but he observed our requirement to speak only when addressed as "Ms. Arendt") to the maximum (a female colleague, playing Franz Kafka, appeared in a pin-striped suit of the 1930s; she adopted a thick German accent and displayed all the personal idiosyncracies of the novelist). Indeed, when Kafka entered coughing consumptively and telling me that he feared groups and was not sure whether he wanted to subject himself to the inquiries of ten demanding students, I myself was unsure, for a few wonderful moments, whether this were the real Kafka or my colleague, who often expressed qualms about entering a classroom. For the ten weeks of the seminar, we talked to the guests exclusively about the first of our seminar topics: the concept of evil. We saw each guest twice, the first time alone, then two weeks later with the guest who had appeared in the intervening week. Imagine what happens when one couples Job with Aquinas or the ebullient Ms. Arendt with the neurotic and withdrawn Kafka. For the final session, the students, who all along had been doing research on the seminar's second topic, the Holocaust, gathered around the table and impersonated—with some overlap, to be sure—one of the guests.

Problems and Outcomes

Such a format has a number of potential pitfalls. How can anyone impersonate someone else? But, for that matter, when I stand behind a lectern giving a supposedly unbiased account of Shakespeare, am I really unbiased? Surely, we would admit that the Shakespeare so presented can be nothing more than Homan's Shakespeare. In effect, we tried to make honest persons out of my colleagues. Can teachers with no formal training as actors really act? We tried to defuse this problem by allowing for the minimal impersonation typified by Ms. Arendt.

But, potential problems are not the same thing as verifiable results. And, what were those results? They were both many and interesting, I believe. My colleagues were productively thrown off stride by the experience. Unable to rely on the normal tactics of teachers—the Socratic method, the authority of the teacher, the planned class hour, the intellectual qualifications of an academic—they were forced to deal with the subject—that is, the object of their impersonation—in a manner that was more direct, more honest, and often more eloquent than normally would be the case. We all knew it was play, but that fact allowed us to play intellectually and at times emotionally with important figures and issues. My observation was—and this was confirmed by my colleagues — that the students retained many more times the information and had a clearer grasp of complex issues than we would usually anticipate. Indeed, the students invited several favorite figures back to the seminar, and these invitations were always accepted. Passions were aroused as fellow teachers, hiding behind a disguise, spoke with each other often at the level of noisy but earnest arguments, with animation, with emotions, defending under the guise of a character beliefs that, when the truth shone through, were curiously close to their own.

When Kafka made a negative reference to Orson Welles's film of his novel *The Trial,* the students asked if we could see that movie before Kafka made a return visit in two weeks. My schedule was riddled with conflicts, so as father of an infant who typically rose at five in the morning, I told the students that the only time I could see *The Trial* with them would be on Monday morning at 5 A.M. So, one Monday at 4:45 A.M., all ten students assembled, bringing coffee and doughnuts. We saw the movie between five and seven, discussed it between seven and nine, then discussed our views of *The Trial* with our guest between nine and eleven. As I recall, no one left the room during those six hours and the conversation was nonstop. As the quarter wore on, the students became very sophisticated in handling the guests and began to incorporate much of what had gone before into their questions, making the parallels and connections between authors, texts, and periods that good teachers hope for and do not always find.

We repeated the format during the winter quarter. This time, our major topic was the concept of power, and our secondary topic was power at the university. Our visitors included Beckett, Hegel, Bismarck (played by the dean of our college), the great Harvard jurisprudential scholar Lon Fuller, Marx, and Lenin.

At the end of the quarter, the students proposed that we broaden the base of our efforts and give a universitywide course with places for two hundred students; the honors students would run the discussion sections. With recent events in Iran and Afganistan in mind, our topic for the large course was war, revolution, and morality, and our guests were the German theologian Dietrich Bonhoeffer, a southern slave holder and an abolitionist, Goethe, Ortega y Gasset, the avant-garde German artist Joseph Beuys, and the French filmmaker Jean-Luc Godard. Even with ten times the number of students and a mixture of freshmen and seniors, the quality of the students' performance (as measured by a major paper), the sophistication of their questions, and the amount of information and ideas generated by the format were about on par with those of the honors students in the seminars. The large spring quarter course was still intimate in a sense, for the students tended to cluster in groups of like minds or preoccupations. Without the lecture format or the questions-and-answers device, the faculty impersonator could address the group as a whole, a segment of the group, or even an individual, since all individuals were subsumed under the general role of host.

At times, the boundary between reality and illusion, between a colleague's speaking with authority about an individual who had been the object of a life's study and that colleague's impersonation of the individual, was productively blurred. When my colleague in sociology, Herman Vera, came in as Ortega complete with silver hair, a European-looking suit, and a thick Spanish accent, he sat on stage behind a desk and, before opening the floor to questions, asked me to read a statement in English translation to the students: The statement said, in effect, that a severe peptic ulcer would force him to sit, rather than stand, for the two hours. Vera or "Ortega" then asked me if I would go to the vending machines outside the lecture hall and bring him back a carton of milk—obviously for the ulcer. Later that day, after his magnificent performance as Ortega, I called Vera to congratulate him but also to express my dismay about his ulcer. He laughed and told me that it was Ortega, not Vera, who had the ulcer—a detail of Ortega's life that a layman could not have known. The French playwright Jean Genêt argues in *The Balcony* that every illusion requires one small touch of reality for its achievement, like the drop of black that painters say can be added to a bucket of white paint to enhance its whiteness. If you will, what happened here was the reverse: I was so caught up with the metadramatics of Vera's playing Ortega that I thought the ulcer was the real-life ingredient that heightened the actor's impersonation.

I suspect that my thesis about classroom as theater and teacher (or student) as performer succeeded for several reasons. The teacher had the same degree of authority, if not more, since the students tended to take their responsibilities as hosts very seriously. But, that authority, under the protective cover of an illusion sustained by actor and audience, was somehow divorced from the authoritarianism against which students often rebel. The text took the form of its author, not of an intermediary in disguise. One of my colleagues, Ronald Carson, confessed that, as he impersonated Dietrich Bonhoeffer, a figure on whom he had spent a lifetime of research, he found himself approaching Bonhoeffer in an entirely new way, because he was forced to speak for and like Bonhoeffer to issues that his real-life prototype would surely have addressed if he had lived in our age.

The students helped to make the illusion take hold by opening up with small talk, then progressing to more important issues, as I suspect we all would if a great writer or philosopher had entered our house or joined our table as an honored guest. Once that illusion was in place, however, we "forgot" that it was merely theater, just as the theater audience forgets when absorbed in a production. For the students, their role was magnified. Not just receptors, not simply students there to learn from someone who already knew the ropes, they had a role as significant as that of the guest, for it was their conversation with the guest, not the actor's monologue, that determined the success or failure of the performaance. If you will, our experiment reversed the title of this chapter, establishing the theater as classroom on the basis of the metaphor of the classroom as theater.

Learning Through Transforming Junk

My fears that technology threatened both teaching and the humanistic principles underlying it led to my second experiment, in which the teacher as director and the students as actors, artists, and audience can use the most visible manifestations of our technology—its waste products, its junk—as materials with which to enhance their imaginative potential and, as a consequence, their own contribution to their education.

We all know that word, language, and text reigned supreme for centuries. This supremacy was most obvious in the medieval school system, before the invention of the printing press. The teacher, standing—in that revealing phrase—at the head of the class, read aloud from a manuscript that his students copied in turn. During this period, the text literally overwhelmed any positive role for either teacher or student. The printing press abolished that function. There was no need for dictation, since every student could own his own printed text. But, a new "text" was substituted. Since the literal text was now everyone's, the focus changed to the text as interpreted, whether by teacher or by priest. The issue became one of how well one perceived a text, and students dutifully learned to interpret the text, to make their own text, from the teacher's example.

But, one might cynically observe that in our video age there is no need for verbal text. Television is an auditory and visual medium that almost renders the written word obsolete. It is not so much a question of whether our students can write as it is of whether they need to write at all. If the day comes when home units capable of transforming speech into written words are within the reach of the average person, the question itself will be moot. Please understand me: This is not the way it is or needs to be. But, given our traditional conception of the teacher's role, I argue that we have not taken full recognition of this technological fact. We use video—sometimes shamelessly: At one university, a large economics course has a single live class with thirty students that is videotaped and then broadcast to the thousand other students in the course. The concept of small classes or even of classroom as theater assumes an irony when the class does not have a live teacher.

But, we now know from television that there are more ways of speaking than through words, and it is precisely the media of minimal speech—television, cinema, rock music—that speak most influentially to our students. How, therefore, might our students speak imaginatively with and through that technology, especially through its seemingly nonmaterialistic opposite, the theater, yet use its ecologically disastrous by-product, junk?

I have used the demonstration described in this section both with an honors class of ten students and with an Introduction to Drama audience of seven hundred. If it is correct to assume that there is an artist in each one of us, the demonstration should work with any group, regardless of age or intellectual level. All that is required is an audience and a pile of junk, the sort of stuff that one can find in an attic or basement—broken garden tools, old baby toys, empty soda cans, materials that one would put into a trash can rather than into a garbage can. Students should be divided into four or five groups. If you are working with seven hundred students, four or five groups of ten students each could represent their classmates. The demonstration has four acts.

Act One. Ask each group of students to pick one piece of junk and, while you are out of the room, to look at that piece and imagine it as something other than what it is. A soda can is not a soda can—you might show, by way of demonstration—but rather an image of the endless cycles of existence, with the hole in the top being the one-way exit for those unfortunate souls who lose their momentum. Used dental floss is a metaphor for the purposelessness that one feels when a love affair is over. And so on. My experience has been that students take everything lightly at this first stage but that that is just the right mood for the sort of creativity that they will be called on to demonstrate as the experiment progresses. Give them five minutes to work out an explanation. When you reenter the room, play the part of an innocent museum visitor who stumbles on a museum not of masterpieces but of junk. As you pick up the soda can and address yourself to the first group's representative, you can say something like this: "Now, this seems not to be art at all but only a soda can." "Oh, no," the student representative replies. "It may look like a soda can, but in reality it is actually"—and then follows the metaphor on which the group has agreed. At this stage, students are probably wondering what the teacher is trying to do. Is this some kind of ice-breaking stunt?

Act Two. This time, before you make your second exit, ask the students to add a second piece to the first, making a collage in effect. Joining the soda can to a toothbrush, one can see it as the cycle of existence; the brush points the way out of the rat race—an alternative to giving up by falling through the hole. Leave the room, return in five minutes, and replay the museum visitor's role. This time, my experience has been, the explanations become more complex and more serious. It is surprising how ingenious students can be, however they fare under traditional academic measurements. The groups will also be closer at this point, working together like an ensemble. It is still junk, but the junk itself is irrelevant at this stage. The issue is: How creatively can we think about these objects that are society's discards?

Act Three. The rules now change. Before you leave, tell each group to pick as many more pieces of junk as it needs to create a large-scale collage extending the two-piece collage of Act Two. But—and here is the difference—when you return, you will require two things of each group: It needs a title for its own large collage—for example, "Existence Without Fizz, or Can or Be Canned"—and it also needs a title for the next group's collage. The second group needs a title for its own collage as well as title for the next group's. The last group must devise titles for its own collage and for the first group's. When you return, ask the first group what title they imagine the second group has given its own collage. When the title is offered, the second group reveals the "proper" title. Very often, you will be delighted by the proximity between the suggested and real titles. Repeat the process down the line, each group first giving the suggested title for the next group, then matching that title with the real title. The actors, if you will, are now functioning also as audience. They are both creating and, through the suggested titles, trying audiencelike to account for someone else's creation.

Act Four. Now that each group knows the proper title of its rival, ask each group to do some automatic writing. That is, as the first group looks at the collage of the second group, one of its members puts the proper title at the top of a sheet of paper; he or she then solicits comments from fellow members on the second group's collage—anything that comes into their heads, without thinking. The result will probably be a poem in black verse. I suggest putting a two-minute deadline on this automatic writing. Then, hold a contest with the students who have remained in the audience. Ask each group, now that the rival group has offered a poetrylike description of its work, to stand behind its collage as the audience renders its judgment through applause. The winning collage is determined by the volume and duration of the applause.

I have found that the results are practically uniform whatever the group and whatever its size or intellectual level. The movement is from lighthearted agreement to play to game to earnest response to a rival group's work. The groups themselves play the role of both actor and audience, teacher and student. And, whatever they imagine their creative potential to be, this experiment generally enhances that concept. I use this exercise to free the minds of English majors before we tackle Renaissance poetry. Despite a half century of New Criticism and attention to the poem as being no less than meaning, even the best students—particularly the high achievers on their way to professional schools—think of poetry not as picture making, not as something at once physical and intellectual, but as little more than versified concepts. I have also used it with freshman drama students as we move from traditional plays to the more experimental plays of the modern theater, to which such terms as *main theme* and *resolution* can no longer be applied: for example, Genêt's *The Maids,* with its purposeful blurring of sham and reality, or Brecht's *Mother Courage* with its evenly balanced dialectics. My demonstration underscores how much the world, even the world of junk, can be transformed by an inquiring and imaginative mind and how collectively, both as audience and as actors, we can transform that world. The link between the external and internal, the physical and the conceptual, the teacher and the student, the actor and the audience is preserved.

Education and Enactment

If for the teacher the written text is challenged by an increasingly visually oriented culture, then perhaps it is the theater, that curious medium combining the verbal and the visual, that represents a new arena for the survival needs of students as well as teachers. The teachers in the course described in the first section of this chapter balanced what they said with how they physically enacted that saying before an audience. Similarly, the theater can be defined as the physical enactment of a verbal, conceptual world. I suggest, with Hamlet, that "thinking makes it so." The experiment with junk shows us that what we see can be determined by what we think or by what we think we see. Seeing the classroom as theater and the teacher as actor obligates the teacher to be an actor, and to be an actor is to teach with both the body and the mind, with both the physical and the verbal. The theatrical term *enactment* underscores this point. Recognizing the physical, visual, nonconceptual half of our selves as humans and as teachers creates a climate in which the classroom, like the theater, seems close to life itself, bound as it is to the physical, to survival, and enhanced as it is by those creatures walking upright who think about their external world and in thinking charge it with meaning, even as they establish an inner world of the spirit.

The atom bomb and the gas oven—the mind that shaped reality through such technological tools represents a negative charge. In calling on other teachers to see the classroom as theater, I am calling for a positive charge to our teaching. The obligation now rests equally on the two halves of that performance, teacher and student, actor and audience. Indeed, those roles often reverse in good classroom theater. Perhaps by thus recharging our teaching can we, as well as our students, survive, and meaningfully so, in the world that we have right now.

Sidney Homan, a Lilly Senior Teaching Fellow (1979–1980)
and Teacher of the Year in the College of Arts and Sciences (1975)
is professor of English at the University of Florida.

Incorporating simple principles of memory theory into classroom lectures and materials enhances involvement, speed, and success in student learning.

Helping Students Remember

Donald K. Fry

My participation in the Fund for the Improvement of Post-Secondary Education (FIPSE) observation project raised my already high consciousness of my own teaching methods and style. In the course of student interviews, I discovered a variety of memory strategies centered on note taking. Most strikingly, one student never wrote down more than five or six words from any class, yet he could easily reconstruct all the ideas, most of the details and examples, and even some parts verbatim. He pictured each session as a tree, and his half dozen words labeled the branches, from which depended all the proceedings of the class. For example, he wrote down five words from a lecture on characterization in *Beowulf: description, speeches, reaction, opposites,* and *monsters;* these nouns branched from a main trunk labeled *Beowulf,* by which the student meant the hero, not the poem. Although he claimed to have invented this technique for himself, it closely parallels the memorizing strategies taught in ancient rhetorical handbooks (Yates, 1966; Post, 1932).

The Schemata of Memory

Most people think of memory as a type of computer taking in bits of data, storing them, and retrieving them as required. But,

J. Katz (Ed.). *Teaching as Though Students Mattered.* New Directions for
Teaching and Learning, no. 21. San Francisco: Jossey-Bass, March 1985.

psychologists generally prefer the model of F. C. Bartlett (1932). Bartlett divides memory processes into perception and recall, proposing that the process of perception itself organizes materials to be memorized into general impressions accompanied by a few striking details, which are both then stored. Such perception patterns vary according to the individual, but there is a counter tendency toward standardized patterns determined by social groups. The material that is easiest to memorize generally has "great structural simplicity, . . . structural regularity, . . . or extreme familiarity" (Bartlett, 1932, p. 45). Bartlett (p. 213) summarizes recall as follows: "Remembering is not the re-excitation of innumerable fixed, lifeless, and fragmentary traces. It is an imaginative reconstruction, built out of the relation of our attitude towards a whole active mass of organized past reactions to experience and to a little outstanding detail which commonly appears in image and language form. It is hardly ever really exact, even in the most rudimentary cases of rote recapitulation." Bartlett calls these internal perception patterns *schemata* and proposes that they interact and change with the demands of particular situations. The collection of schemata and outstanding details forms a highly organized and dynamic mass that we label *memory*. The mind does not store this organized perceived material as discrete units; rather, it connects stored elements.

The efficiency of memory depends on the organization not just of individual items but also of groups of memorized items (Kintsch, 1970). Truly efficient structures involve links formed in storage (James, 1890). George Miller's (1956) brilliant notion of *chunking* accounts for some concentrative structures. Miller discovered that seven units, give or take two, fill the memory, so that efficient perception often involves consolidation of recoding within units. For example, if we need to remember a forty-nine-digit number, we may think of it as seven telephone numbers, each broken down further into a three-digit and a four-digit unit. Chunking reduces effort (Miller and others, 1960).

Most memorizers untrained in memory systems simply repeat material until it sticks in their minds. Repetition takes several forms: speaking the material aloud, "speaking" the material internally, and repeated recall. Repeated recall associates the material with different contexts, increasing its links in storage (Hunter, 1964). But, mere repetition does not cause memorization in the absence of interest and attention, nor does repetition necessarily lead to memorization if there is not an intent to learn. Lyon (1917, p. 7) captures this principle nicely: "Interest is one of the main factors to be considered in memory; it is the mother of attention, and attention is the mother of memory."

In summary, as the effort required to perceive and store

material decreases, so does the effort needed to retain and recall it. The mind has its structures in individual and cultural forms; memories last as they approximate those forms. Material should have maximum associations with known materials, and frequent recall maximizes new associations. Material should contain rich chunks of information in units of four or five groups: "Anything which makes an item 'stand out' from the others is memorized soonest and becomes a distinctive reference point around which the remainder of the memorizing task is organized" (Hunter, 1964, p. 137). Concrete visual imagery also helps, since it involves another sense. The structure should convey some idea of a whole and of the relation of parts to the whole. Finally, the memorizer should hear the structure recited orally, daily and complete.

Memory, Organization, and Learning

I teach Anglo-Saxon and Middle English literature in two forms, small translation classes and large lectures. In the former, students learn a language they already know in part, since Old English contains many cognates with modern English, but its Germanic grammar is inflected. For example, I modify the paradigm of third-person pronouns from a standard textbook (Mitchell, 1968) so that looks like this:

	Masculine	*Neuter*	*Feminine*	*Plural*
Nominative	*he*	*hit*	heo	hie
Accusative	hine	*hit*	hie ⟷ hie	
Genitive	*his* ⟷ his	*hire*	hira	
Dative	*him* ⟷ him	*hire*	him	

Students learn this pattern very quickly if they perceive the italicized forms as sounding essentially like their modern equivalents. Three of the four plural forms sound something like modern ones without the preceding *th* sound, the neuter genitive and dative singular are the same as the masculine, and so on. The student needs to pay special attention to only four of the sixteen forms: masculine accusative, feminine nominative and accusative, and plural accusative. The visual highlights allow this paradigm to slip easily into the learner's mind. The process uses the principles of multiple senses (sight and sound), repetition, peaks of attention, and relating the new to the familiar. This visual device for rote memorization of details epitomizes the further application of these principles for remembering larger patterns of ideas.

Mnemonic devices have played an important role in formal teaching and everyday learning since man first learned to talk. Everyone knows "Thirty days hath September," and medieval learners could keep their moral aims straight with couplets like this one: "Kepe well X, and flee from VII; rule well V, and come to heven" (Luria and Hoffman, 1974, p. 122). The Roman numerals signify respectively the ten Commandments, the seven deadly sins, and the five senses, which all encode complex views on behavior. The seven deadly sins, for example, serve as a checklist for confessors, a summary of behaviors to avoid, and a key to moral psychology. Categorizing human behavior in such simple terms might seem reductive if we lose sight of the pictures and stories associated with each sin in popular literature. But, remembering gluttony at once as a sow and as a fat slob who cannot pass a tavern on his way to church cements the abstraction in the mind and posts a moral sentinel for symptoms of such behavior in ourselves. Miller's (1956) notion of chunking explains the power of this device. The poem encodes three sets of moral numbers, which in turn encode and compress religious and psychological schemas. Rote memorization has become distinctly unfashionable in education, although it still plays an ancillary role, especially in language and science instruction. We distinguish memorizing from remembering, although the underlying principles remain the same. We should keep in mind that creative thinking involves not only the recall of subject matter but also the recall of processes and modes of judgment (Hunt, 1982). Still, range and precision of thinking depend, among other factors, on the extent of storage and the accuracy of perception.

In my lecture classes, organization of the lecture helps students to remember probably more than any other factor. I discovered that most of my students contrasted sharply with the student cited earlier: They took chaotic notes, jotting down facts, jokes, and page numbers in a course explicitly designed to teach judgment and analysis. I perceived the gulf between the intentions of my lecture organization and the students' note taking. Many of the students devised strategies to serve what I call semester memory, which keeps the material in their heads until ten seconds after the final examination, while I hoped to lodge techniques for understanding literature permanently in their minds. The course material would survive beyond December or May only if strong reference points organized the surrounding matter into memorable units. So, in subsequent semesters I altered my lecture style to provide these needed reference points ready-made. Lectures became mountain ranges with peaks organizing the valleys.

In my experience, students show little skill in recognizing the most important ideas in a lecture unless they receive some guided high-lighting. Most teachers intuitively highlight by repetition. I once quipped that anyone can spot professors, because they say everything three times. Actually, few professors perceive themselves as saying the same things over and over again. Mere repetition is not nearly so effective as repetition with variation, because the variations increase the contexts by which students can retrieve stored materials.

Many commentators have noticed that effective teachers tend to tell jokes and anecdotes and even to act out matters visually. At least every five years, some academic showman gains national attention by wearing costumes to class or by imitating famous scientists or authors. Such impersonating helps to create a friendly atmosphere that is conducive to learning, and it also creates a certain tone of attractive humility on the instructor's part. But, I also find that jokes, anecdotes, and gestures tend to stick firmly in the audience's minds, providing "points" for organized memory. Students of famous performing professors, such as George Lyman Kittredge, can always remember anecdotes, but they can also usually recall the professor's ideas as well. Ideally, the intellectual peaks, clearly marked, should coincide with the visual and humorous peaks. Pinnacled peaks organize wider valleys. I recently tested this principle with an average student, asking her if she remembered the arguments used by the absurd debating chickens in Chaucer's Nun's Priest's Tale, which I had highlighted in a lecture more than a year earlier. She recalled my observation that Dame Pertelote's name, pronounced aloud in Middle English with a staccato rhythm and bubbling vowels, sounds very like a hen clucking. She laughed when she recalled the slight wing flutter I gave with my hands as I clucked shamelessly in front of the class. She then recalled the arguments of both chickens in detail. The visual and aural spectacle focused her memories of detailed and abstract trains of thought, just as William James (1890) argued.

Personal applications can achieve much the same effect. I often spin tales about my ferocious archeologist wife to make a point about women stick in the minds of class members. But, applications to their own lives prove even more effective. Spinning scenarios requiring empathy and common sense cements complex viewpoints, making them seem familiar. For example, to explain and capture the operational wit of Odysseus, I often ask students to picture themselves in the hero's situation: "You've been away almost twenty years, fighting a war and trying to sail home. You are shipwrecked, and you spend three nights in the sea swimming to stay alive. Just when you are about to give up and drown you see land and swim ashore, only to fall asleep.

The next morning, you wake up naked, covered with dirt and leaves and salt, unshaven and utterly lost. You find yourself face to face with a beautiful princess, and the first words out of your mouth will determine whether she calls armed guards or welcomes you to her father's palace. What would you say?" No student, no professor, no hero could improve on what Odysseus does say: "Mistress, please, are you divine or mortal?" He goes on to hint about marriage, and she welcomes him (Lattimore, 1965, p. 117). But, I paraphrase his reply: "Oh, you're so beautiful, you must be a goddess." I give my hair a pat, raise my voice an octave, and reply: "Oh, do you think so?" This gesture and focused words peak the moment in their memories, and the scene itself serves as a key to remembering many other instances of Odysseus's cunning. Such devices of empathy can put students on the cliff looking at Grendel's pool through Beowulf's eyes or helping the Wife of Bath's rapist knight to save his life with the proper feminist sentiment. Such moments stick with us, and the complex ideas around them cling in organized memory.

Besides such familiarization and marking, lecturers can also enhance remembering by simple and perceptible organization. Structures can be as simple as the old preacher's formula: "First you tell 'em what you gonna tell 'em; then you tell 'em; and then you tell 'em what you done told 'em." (Have you ever wondered why that old chestnut usually appears in dialect? The dialect conjures up the picture of the country preacher, making the triplet more memorable.) We often hear a speaker praised because the seams don't show. However, such praise refers to the performance, not to the audience's recall. In my opinion, the teacher should let the structures show, highlighting the theses, transitions, and repetitions. A memorable lecture should resemble a Gothic cathedral, with the ribs and buttresses soaring before our eyes. At the simplest level, the instructor can write a short outline on the board. The lecturer can begin with a list of main points and pause in the middle for a retrospective. Every television police show has a scene just beyond the middle commercials where the angry lieutenant chews out the heroes and in so doing reviews the plot and the cast of characters: "Now, you listen to me, Hutch: First you hit that Staunton dame, and then. . ." The instructor should indicate transitions clearly but simply, using such phrases as "moving to my third point" or "clucking right along." Every lecture should end with an ending, which couples a glance back at the ground covered with a sneak preview of the next lesson.

I choose the lecture method when I want to convey complex material accurately, quickly, and memorably to a large group in a mode attuned to their level of understanding at the moment. I want what is in my head to arrive inside their heads and stay there, where it remains ready for active use and further development. Depending totally on their idiosyncratic organization of heard materials guarantees forgetting. As Bartlett (1932) says, audience members inevitably perceive and store material by recasting it into their own schemas anyway, but powerful structures should work against distortion, at least to some degree. The techniques described here draw on the performance side of ancient rhetoric and analogously reflect the structures of modern fiction and art. Good teachers and good lecturers often think of themselves as poets of a sort, and the rewards are the same: momentary applause and lasting memory.

References

Bartlett, F. C. *Remembering: A Study in Experimental and Social Psychology.* Cambridge, England: Cambridge University Press, 1932.

Hunt, M. "How the Mind Works." *New York Times Magazine,* 24 January 1982, pp. 30–33, 47–48, 50, 52, 64, 68.

Hunter, I. M. L. *Memory.* Harmondsworth, England: Pelican Books, 1964.

James, W. *Principles of Psychology.* New York: Holt, 1890.

Kintsch, W. *Learning, Memory, and the Conceptual Process.* New York: Wiley, 1970.

Lattimore, R. (Trans.). *The Odyssey of Homer.* New York: Harper & Row, 1965.

Luria, M. S., and Hoffman, R. L. (Eds.). *Middle English Lyrics.* New York: Norton, 1974.

Lyon, D. O. *Memory and the Learning Process.* Baltimore: Warwick and York, 1917.

Miller, G. A. "The Magical Number Seven, Plus or Minus Two: Some Limits on Our Capacity for Processing Information." *Psychological Review,* 1956, *63,* 81–97.

Miller, G. A., Galanter, E., and Pribram, K. H. *Plans and the Structure of Behavior.* New York: Holt, Rinehart and Winston, 1960.

Mitchell, B. *A Guide to Old English.* Oxford, England: Blackwell, 1968.

Post, L. A. "Ancient Memory Systems." *Classical Weekley,* 1932, *25,* 105–109.

Yates, F. A. *The Art of Memory. Chicago: University of Chicago Press, 1966.*

Donald K. Fry is associate director of the Poynter Institute for Media Studies in St. Petersburg, Florida.

Student growth and change during the college years can be described as either evolutionary or revolutionary. They are influenced by career orientation, activities, role models, and friendships.

Challenge and Support for Student Growth

Karen H. Nelson

The abundance of research and theory regarding adolescent and adult development has created a sound basis for the study of college students. However, precise study is made increasingly difficult by the number of variables necessary to explain behavior and by the difficulty inherent in identifying the variables that are the most important to measure. My own experience as a developmental psychologist, teacher, and adviser has led me to a resolution of these difficulties. My purpose here is to discuss how salient events influence the development of differences in my students. My central characters are Frank and Lori. Frank is a talented person and a frustrating student, characterized by gradual, predictable change. Lori would have flunked out of college had she not changed, and she changed dramatically. These students were selected on the basis of profiles from the Omnibus Personality Inventory (OPI). Personal interviews provided validation for my interpretation of OPI profiles.

Transition: Evolution or Revolution

Frank and Lori repeated the OPI almost a year and a half after they had originally taken it. At first glance, Frank's profiles were very

J. Katz (Ed.). *Teaching as Though Students Mattered.* New Directions for Teaching and Learning, no. 21. San Francisco: Jossey-Bass, March 1985.

similar, whereas Lori's profiles were dramatically different. Frank exemplifies evolution, Lori, revolution, but it may not always be that way for these two young people. It may be that, as we grow and change, we follow both patterns, but at different times, under different pressures. I am interested in how I can respond most effectively to students undergoing these different kinds of transition. When the OPI was administered for the second time, Frank was a senior anticipating a career in theater. He was amiable although part of a nonconformist clique. He has strong political commitments and a clear sense of his strengths and weaknesses. While he was an accomplished performer and a bright student, his extracurricular commitments sometimes interfered with academic success. Frank's second profile showed greater interests in esthetic activities, greater cognitive complexity, and better impulse control. The changes were predictable and more quantitative than qualitative; they were beneficial, consistent with his personal and professional goal; and his style was simply becoming more distinct, as one would expect with increasing maturity.

Lori was a sophisticated young woman, usually cheerful and friendly. When she first took the OPI, she was a freshman, and, like 40 percent of our incoming freshmen, she aspired to be a doctor. By the end of her first semester, Lori's premedical plans were in question. She was not doing well academically, she did not like the courses she was taking, and she did not feel very good about herself. As her adviser, I talked with her at length about courses to take in the spring and encouraged experimentation. She took psychology, sociology, second-semester biology, and a required cultural heritage course. At the end of her first year, she had obtained a D, a D – , and an F in biology and chemistry, B's in English, psychology, and sociology, and a C in the heritage course. Her grade point average (GPA) was 1.86. Her GPA for the fall of her sophomore year was 3.00. Lori's revolution occurred in the intellectual and career orientations of her personal style. She shifted from having dominant interests in intellectual activities consistent with an undergraduate concentration in the natural sciences and a career in medicine to a style consistent with a concentration on social science or humanities. The shift was abrupt and qualitative. Lori's style has become harder to describe, more ambiguous and puzzling than it was before. Her changes in style have been accompanied by a loss of stability, a loss of career orientation, and the emergence of an exploratory view of an academic major and future career. Her revolution parallels Piaget's disequilibration process in that it involves a rejection of prior structures or style, a period of confused, searching behavior, and a resolution with emergence of a new structure only as the individual constructs it herself (Flavell, 1977).

Lori's freshman year experiences presented her with the image of a student who failed at the things she thought she did well and who did well at the things with which she had little experience. Frank's junior year brought no comparable surprises. Frank could evolve because he did not need to do anything else to progress toward his goals. Lori underwent revolution in the face of major challenges to her premedical goals. With a GPA of 1.86, she needed to do something intellectually and do it quickly. The two had different views of risk. Frank's OPI data indicate greater independence and an openness to risk and anxiety; Lori's profile suggests greater conformity and low risk taking. I guess that Frank permitted change to occur, whereas Lori tried to forestall growth until revolutionary change was the only alternative to academic failure. If one is afraid to permit the transition to occur, one is likely to deny, escape, or avoid acknowledgement of the need to change. There may be little relationship between kind of change and openness to change. Revolution often occurs because the individual has not been willing or able to evolve and adapt to demands placed on him or her.

The greatest risk for the individual undergoing evolutionary change is complacency and stagnation. To protect Frank from cutting off options, he needed to continue to use his existing skills and to be exposed to new challenges. Lori adopted an experimental attitude as a means of facilitating her transition. What she needed was validation that failure is okay as long as you learn from it and reassurance that she was fundamentally competent enough to undergo the transition. While the evolving student needs stimulation and occasional prodding, the student facing revolution needs moral support, some expression of confidence that he or she can and will weather the crisis, as well as someone who will listen, support, and sometimes protect. If the student undergoing revolutionary change is overstimulated or prodded too much, he or she may pull back and escape or avoid the transition. At the same time, to praise and coddle the student who is evolving slowly is to invite arrogance, stagnation, and complacency. Frank had a habit of falling behind in his work, requesting extensions or incompletes and ultimately failing to submit the work altogether, for which he received F's. He seemed to fall prey to complacency, letting things slide until it was too late unless he was confronted and prodded. Lori, in contrast, needed to leave her failures behind her. Had I attempted to convince her to retake the courses she had failed and to try harder, or study more, or socialize less, I might have lost her trust and so damaged her self-esteem that she would become resigned to failure. In attempting to differentiate student needs for support or challenge, we can understand our students better and help them to understand themselves better by asking such questions as these: What changes do you see in yourself in the last year? How do you feel about your academic record, your career plans, your place in this college? Do you have a tendency to respond impulsively, sometimes making stupid mistakes, or are you the opposite, sometimes being so reluctant to act that you miss important opportunities? Detecting patterns of evolution and revolution is important for the student, and it has benefits for the institution.

The mistake of treating developmental transitions as pathological phenomena is widespread. I am convinced that more students have had their transition undone by benevolent advisers who focused on the elimination of frustration, confusion, and depression than have received the delicate balance of challenge and support that I see as desirable.

It is worth noting that, when Lori shifted her energy allocation to intellectual matters, she became more wary of the complex and the frustrating. It is as if the demands for substantial intellectual growth in formal operational, self-reflective, analytic, and synthetic skills were temporarily overwhelming. She can use her skills, and she is learning new ones, but she fares best when the tasks that she confronts are simple. She needs the opportunity to exercise her newfound skills without the demand of highly sophisticated material or the fear of significant failure. There are many Loris in our classes. We all know those who will get A's in our disciplines despite what we do and those who will do badly no matter what we do. The Loris start out with C's and low B's, but they have the potential to achieve B+'s and A's. They do not need coddling or condescension. They need honest feedback about the skills they have and the skills they lack. They need our praise when they succeed and our encouragement when they do not. If we overpraise or fail to challenge them, they will lose respect for us and confidence in themselves. Not surprisingly, the same results accrue if we overcriticize and overload. In the spring of her sophomore year, Lori found biology easy when it had been her nemesis the year before.

Change Agents

Change agents are the salient experiences during the college years that can serve to prompt movement. In this section, I will discuss four factors influencing change: career orientation, activities, role models, and friendships.

Career orientation can serve to direct the course that a student takes in a positive way, or it can prompt foreclosure. Frank provides an example of positive impact. His identification of a career was accompanied by both intellectual growth and emotional stability. Frank has high needs for autonomy, low interest in altruistic and practical concerns, and little interest in analytical, scientific endeavors. In his junior year, his profile seemed to preclude medicine, law, business, education, and human services. In his senior year, his humanities orientation and flexible emotional style combined with his other qualities to support a career in theater design. One can speculate that selecting a career gave him the sense of personal integration necessary both to grow intellectually and to curb impulsiveness. Lori illustrates the negative effects of career selection. For her, the critical step in career orientation was from foreclosure—a premature commitment to medicine—to flexibility. In a large university, she might well have preserved her dualism, her low intellectual interests, and her foreclosure. The emphasis of our college on liberal arts enabled her to explore, to get close supervision and clear feedback from professors, and to have a diverse support system of students and faculty members. Freeing herself from premature career commitment freed her emotionally and enhanced her intellectual interests. She is exploring career options and recognizes that she has a long way to go.

Activities are less mandatory than career decision making. Career orientation is often quite consistent with course work and demands little additional time, while activities are time-consuming and may conflict with course-related activities. Activities are sometimes deemed secondary. Yet, because activities are chosen, they help to identify where and how energy is being allocated. A critical choice for Lori may have been not to join a sorority in her freshman year, which might have supported her extroverted yet foreclosed and conformist personal style.

The critical question is how the student benefits from the role that an activity creates. A fundamental benefit accrues from having multiple roles, which contribute to both role confusion and identity attainment. By experiencing oneself as a student, employee, athlete, and sorority member, one begins to see the importance of integrity and flexibility. Foreclosure of an activity-defined role—for example, jock, actor, or Young Republican—is just as damaging as foreclosure of an academic or career role—for example, premed, philosopher, or schoolteacher. When energy is being deployed in a healthy way, there should be some evidence of synergy: Energy expenditure creates energy; the activity is not perceived as sapping one's strength. Frank shows both the positive and negative aspects of activities. They have been salient in shaping his personal and intellectual development, yet they interfere with personal responsibility and academic life. Given the parallels between extracurricular interests and the qualities that affect learning style, it is sometimes easier to assess developmental status in these domains than it is in course-related domains. The student may also be more willing to experiment in the less risky world of activities.

People who function as role models often have characteristics that attract students with similar characteristics. Several cognitive style researchers advocate a match between the styles of students and teachers, clients and counselors, advisees and advisers. Many practitioners and some institutions have adopted this approach, yet I remain skeptical. Given the tremendous number of dimensions of the self, what should we use as the basis for the match? Should we use intellectual style, or affective style, or both? And, if we do, just because a student who matches my style likes me better than he or she likes a mismatched professor, does that mean that the student will learn more or more easily? In my experience, no single match works to explain my successes and failures with students. Among the students who match my style on any given instrument, some are bright, exciting, friendly, and easy to like, while others are dull, boring, unfriendly, or very easy to dislike. Conversely, some of the students who differ most dramatically from me have been the brightest, most exciting, and most influenced intellectually by me as a role model. What shall I use as my criterion of role modeling? If I ask who writes flattering letters, who stays in touch after graduation, or who comes to the office to talk about personal or career interests, the data fail to explain those for whom I have been a role model, much less how or why. These students chose to value some fragment of a role I play, and they benefit by it.

Role models are important to students. However, to incorporate the concept of role modeling systematically into student development entails three risks. First, role models must be chosen by the student on the basis of what is salient for him or her. Second, role models are most effective when they are transitory. Too often, becoming a role model is accompanied first by arrogance on the part of the role model, then by an attempt to encourage the student to become a clone. One assumes that the student has chosen to emulate the model in all respects, rather than to focus on the salient quality that attracts the student's attention in the first place. The third risk involves the inequity in power between role model and student. Even when the role model has been chosen, he or she often has considerable institutional and emotional authority, for it is the teacher who assigns grades and provides feedback to the student about competence. To institutionalize a matching system is to place students in situations in which they often become very confused about their responsibilities to their role models.

Another relationship, the close friendship, may merit conversion from a haphazard to a deliberate role in students' lives. In close friendships, the egalitarian quality is critical; each friend views the other with respect but as an equal. The first time I recognized this kind of relationship was when two women appeared after the class in which they had learned how to interpret their own OPI profiles. Ann and Rhonda wanted to know what it meant if two profiles were virtually identical. Ann's and Rhonda's enthusiasm intrigued me. They asked questions in and out of class, attended activities that were intellectually stimulating, and often alluded to conversations with one another. Although they were now "best friends" and virtually identical in style, they had not always been. Ann's emotional style opened up after she became close to Rhonda, who was much more open at the outset of their relationship. Now, Rhonda is undergoing significant changes, and Ann provides stability for her. To the extent that I have been able to detect dominance by one partner, there seems always to be some compensatory subordination in some other domain or in the same domain at some other time. In some ways, these friendships create a match in cognitive style for their members. The match is chosen, as it must be in the case of role models, and the relationship is truly equal.

As I pursued my study of friendships, one of my first realizations was the pleasure that students got from exploring their relationships. Recently, when I examined close to thirty friendships, I discovered that a less common but equally important pattern is one of intentional mismatch in friends' styles. In these pairs, the OPI profiles are virtual mirror images in many respects. The friends have chosen one another on the basis of complementarity, not of similarity. Yet, in the few cases on which I had longitudinal data, there were typically some shifts toward congruity. For example, if one friend was initially very low in intellectual complexity and the other very high, a year and a half later they were similar in complexity. If one was very gregarious and the other was introverted and shy, there was a shift toward moderation. It appeared that these shifts toward congruity were defined by the needs of the friendship. If I study with you, our frustration tolerance needs to be similar; if I socialize with you, our social instincts need to merge to some degree, or else I will be the life of the party, while you will be the wallflower. Like careers, activities, and role models, friendships can be change agents for evolution or revolution.

Adult friendships do not persist unless the other provides a distinct stimulation. In the case of the matched friends, the initial stimulation is one of understanding. The typical comment is: "My friend is someone who understands me better than I understand myself." Each friend grows through the other. While such friendships can become incestuous and deter growth, in most cases they do not. Once one sees the other as a vehicle to self-confidence and growth, and once the other reciprocates, the friends begin to explore their differences. Ann, who had never danced before in her life, began to study dance with Rhonda, who had fifteen years of experience. Rhonda, who had hated lab courses, took a course on computer-based education and did beautifully. Partnerships highlight the importance of choice; we choose our friends. Partnerships illustrate a critical mechanism in support systems: We need others to listen and bolster our egos when we are down but to prod us when we feel like staying down.

My explorations of students often result in more questions than answers, and that pleases me. I have discovered that style grows and changes as a function of salient internal and external events. I can reject notions of style and replace them with my notions of evolution and revolution. I can avoid motivation constructs that focus on uncontrollable needs or drives and focus instead on choice. Since transition requires emotional and motivational qualities as well as intellectual ones, I can engage in close examination of the interaction between the cognitive and the affective domains. Like those interactions, concepts of match and mismatch in style suggest strategies for stimulating learning and development in ourselves and others. I am learning to ask better questions of students and advisees, to trust their abilities to define what is important to them, and to value and validate the wealth of experience that their college lives provide.

Reference

Flavell, J. H. *Cognitive Development.* Englewood Cliffs, N.J.: Prentice-Hall, 1977.

*Karen H. Nelson is a professor of psychology
at Austin College, Sherman, Texas.*

College students want teachers who show authority, not of a tyrannical kind but the kind that comes from knowing one's stuff and from the discipline of life itself.

Freedom and Discipline

Ronald Boling

Prefatory Note

In the final stages of preparing this volume, the editor requested the authors to ask their undergraduate students to describe some typical classroom learning experiences. The following essay was the best one received. It was written by a graduate teaching assistant who largely reports about his experiences as an undergraduate. His approach is different from that of the other contributors. However, it shows a young instructor struggling with the central problem of freedom and discipline, those poles around which Whitehead (1967) discussed human learning. The student's description of the "morass of confusion" in which most of his undergraduate English courses left him is poignant and one for any teacher to ponder. In his postscript, the editor discusses some implications of Ronald Boling's essay.

*   *   *

When I belonged to a crop of first-time teaching assistants, our supervisor, a nurturing, earth-mother type, advised us not to call our students by their last names and not to seat them alphabetically in class. Her rationale was that freshmen need some respite from university depersonalization and that they can find a forum for their own ideas in

J. Katz (Ed.). *Teaching as Though Students Mattered.* New Directions for Teaching and Learning, no. 21. San Francisco: Jossey-Bass, March 1985.

a more intimate environment. So, there we were, novice teachers terrified by the certainty of our own inadequacy, slavishly following formulas
(narration, description, classification, definition) that would liberate
these silently staring souls in blue jeans. Impelled by terror, I carried
the Great Liberal Bluff even farther, having the students address me by
my first name, giving them complete freedom (that is, no guidance) on
paper topics, and conducting a humorous, story-filled, and confes-
sional class. Showtime. I gave lots of B's, like a blanket pardon.

Of course, my approach undermined the intent of grammar lectures and the study of rhetorical modes, the intent being to balance
freedom of expression with discipline or, in freshman literature courses,
with scholarship. Having seen repeatedly the facade of freshman maturity vanish after rush week, I have become convinced of the need for
discipline, and having seen freshmen caught in this dilemma—"Sure,
you may write about whatever you like, just so the rhetorical mode is
the most effective means conceivable for presenting your ideas"—I suspect that freedom of expression and scholarly responsibility should be
goals of separate, required courses.

I was fortunate enough to have a freshman composition professor who helped students to earn the ability to communicate freely and
well, and as a junior I had a teacher who gave me a first-rate introduction to scholarship. They are separate disciplines, and I was introduced
to them in the proper order. Fred Rodewald, my freshman comp. professor, always gave us the same assignment. Every two weeks we turned
in a paper on no particular topic of no particular length. Such was the
assignment on day one. Nobody whined shamelessly for more specifics,
because Rodewald had memorized our names before our eyes and
already addressed us all, without the roll, by *Mister* and our last names.
So, we knew he meant at least five pages, and I doubt that he received a
single treatise on cafeteria food or the competing claims of dorm and
home life. I never wrote less than eight pages, in small, male handwrit-
ing. My first piece was titled "A Parental God"; in it I argued that (the
Baptist) God has both paternal and maternal qualities. Although the
piece is lost to posterity, I'm sure I argued for a severance from some
sort of God/parent tyranny. That's freedom of expression, when an
adolescent can work out his wretchedness in intellectual fasion. I worked
hard on the paper and expected an A, but I got a B + , because I hadn't
documented my Biblical passages. I was hurt, but when I saw everyone
else in shock with D's and F's, and when Rodewald patiently explained
that the later papers would be weighted more than the earlier ones and
that we simply had to improve the precision of our prose and the effectiveness of our argumentation, I understood the game plan. Little did I

realize that Rodewald himself always used an effective parenting technique, for a child is never more apt to listen and learn than in the intimate aftermath of deserved discipline.

Rodewald slaughtered our papers. The words *logic* and *evidence?* were a perennial chorus. Simply, he taught us argumentation, regardless of topic or viewpoint. We spent a lot of time discussing essays in our *Borzoi,* always asking if a piece made sense, if it was logical, if statements were accurate or precise, if we believed or agreed with the author. Rodewald spoke often of the authority of the writer, of how he or she sustains or undermines it, and of the contract, the inherent agreement between reader and writer that the writer promises in his thesis. Seldom have I had English courses in which I learned more about meaning than about acceptable style.

I wrote several papers of a political nature while Rodewald and I argued about the difference between a B + and an A – . My problem was that I often left logical gaps between sentences. Taunting adolescent that I was, I soon produced a paper of ponderous, almost medieval, order and pace that forced him to capitulate. A good student will eventually force a break with a teacher he loves or respects, alas, with more violence than grace. I moved into a series of rock album reviews, forcing Rodewald into an alien and hostile world. Young fool that I was, I took all the rope that he gave me. There bloomed a most cankerous blossom, a sixteen-page analysis of a morbid and suicidal narrative rock album. It is not only the frequency of assignments that militates against excessive length; it is also the experience of laboriously creating one's own desert in which one wanders like an Israelite. I cringed with good reason when Rodewald handed back the papers. He'd gleefully whacked out a paragraph here, a page there, shuffled my paragraphs like a deck of cards, criticized the inadequate exposition and definition, and implored me repeatedly to make a point. He called my bluff. I became less ambitious and more precise.

We never had grammar lectures. Instead, Rodewald fielded questions about his corrections, giving us as much detail and as many examples as we wanted. Since we always knew our goal—clarity, logic, evidence—and since we were continually learning improvements, nearly everyone made steady progress. This goal, this sense of an objective referent, seems crucial in undergraduate classes, because the main problem I've noticed in English classes is that students don't know what is expected of them. A professor perceived as too subjective (and ultimately as whimsical) is condemned to disrespect and oblivion.

With Rodewald and Abernethy (the other professor I want to discuss), a student never had to guess what they wanted, because they never put anyone in that position. The perception of an objective standard, illusory or not, rendered their occasional whims all the more imposing, because these guys communed with the gods. They knew so much, Rodewald a continual stream of articulate analysis, Abernethy an endless fountain of knowledge, and their game was so clearly defined, that you could always navigate in their sea (and, satisfied, make port at the bell). They both earned the students' acclamation. I hope to earn such accolades myself some day.

The sad fact is that in most English classes you direct your efforts to figuring out how to play the prof's game, and the result is that you don't learn as much as you should. Perhaps a good indicator of the effectiveness of a course is what you can remember from it. All I remember from our death waltz through the Norton British Lit. was that the crone pronounced *Christianity* "Krist–ya–ayn–uh–tee." That's all I remember, except for certain pornographic and caricatural sketches by my neighbor. One poetry prof never looked down at us, as if a cloud had descended on the class. He was out in the gyres, and so was I, but we never met. In Utopian Lit., the prof drew all over the board for an hour. No one had any idea what he was talking about. His answers to our questions were very long; in fact, the only way we knew he had finished his answer was that he would suddenly pronounce a sentence one word at a time, and his blue eyes would get misty. After being stung with a B – on the first test, I tried a desperation move: I simply redefined every question and then wrote endless diatribes about what I knew.

In one survey course, we took leisurely, sentimental, and voyeuristic strolls through many a poem and play, and this prof kept talking about flowers, since gardening was his hobby. Tests consisted of 100 fill-in-the-blank questions, but the questions were far more serious than anything we did in class, and he proved that you can ask some pretty flaky "objective" questions, as students always observe among themselves. His game was easy, though, since I already knew how to read. My transformational grammar class could have been exciting, and it was good as far as it went, but the prof taught down to the level of the giggling, terrified education majors. His game was too well-defined, too obvious, too easy. He was an eighteenth-century man. An American Lit. prof, my favorite prof but not the best teacher I had, was so depressed at the mediocrity of students that he never really knew what to say in class. He was soft-voiced, slow-starting, and subtle but very good once he got going. Still, his classes lacked continuity. He also let me go way too far with Kerouac, Ginsberg, and Burroughs, and it was only later that I realized that they were frauds.

Anyway, Francis Abernethy introduced me to scholarship. Although his Shakespeare and folklore courses overlap a bit in my memory, what he taught me stands out clearly to this day. On day one, the tall, lean, leathery Texan moved everyone, seating us alphabetically, and he always called us by our last names only: "Boling." We were here not to express ourselves but to learn. The first thing Ab taught us was how to read a play, and he nailed us in class on lecture material: "All right, Boling, what're the criteria for evaluating story and plot?" "Story is evaluated on the basis of suspense and plot on the basis of logic." "That's right." And, he would then apply the principle to the scene at hand. We learned the basics first — a character's depth, function, motivation, conflict, change; a scene's function, obstacles, and dramatic tension; directorial interpretation, exposition, climax, anagnorisis, peripety, denouement, social order — and we applied everything to the play at hand. At least every other class, Ab would say, "All right, get out a sheet," and we'd have six or seven minutes to write a paragraph (he defined *paragraph* the first five times we wrote) on a very specific question that applied a principle to an unannounced aspect of the play. This question would be the starting point of his lecture, and the quizzes, plus an exam or two and a paper, comprised the course grade. Between the quizzes and that itchy silence when he called on you and you turned stupid and red, you tended to prepare for class. However, that brief sting of embarrassment never kept me from his class even if I was unprepared, because his lectures were marvelous. I missed only one class in two semesters — I remember this fact after seven years.

One of his maxims was *everything's folklore.* Endlessly, he spun tales out of words or lines or situations in Shakespeare — Biblical allusions, Greek myths, Euro-American legends, historical anecdotes, etymologies, modern folkloric equivalents (games, institutions, courting rituals, musical forms). He was fascinating. How many teachers would ask each row of students to hum a different note so as to mimic the music of the spheres — and get immediate compliance? How many would illustrate a dactyl by waltzing across the front of the room? Ab stressed that art was mankind's record of itself, a record continued and vivified in human activity itself. We had a sense of an external referent to which Ab himself deferred — mankind. His system of learning seemed divinely ordained or at least benevolently disposed and thus safe, yet it was open-ended, challenging, and worth a lifetime of devotion.

Both Rodewald and Abernethy seemed to promote an objective or external standard toward which one strove. There was something bigger out there to which they themselves were subject, or so it seemed to a young mind. There was never any question of trying to tell them what they wanted to hear. They were guides, not petty tyrants. The field in which they operated was not their turf but open to all who had the discipline and the desire to explore it themselves. With freedom comes responsibility, taught Rodewald. Sure, you can write about anything you want, and you can "discover yourself" in the process, but you have an obligation to your reader, and you should have respect for your own ideas. And for Ab, scholarship was exciting, a way of learning what men say, think, and do; a way of learning from those complementary, contrapuntal processes, art and life. In all my undergraduate English career, these men stand out, not quite alone, from a morass of forgotten confusion.

Editor's Postscript

The theme of the competing claims of freedom and discipline sounded by Ronald Boling is an important one. Interestingly enough, he would like to "require" both. It is widely held belief that students left to their own devices would not necessarily act in their own best interests, that they would not work freely toward their own freedom. Many students share this belief. From one coast to the other, they ask for coercion in order to get students to work. Thus, a mathematics-science sophomore at Harvey Mudd College in California writes: "Many people might object to practices such as graded quizzes and assigned graded homework, insisting that a student should perform only for the love of learning. Such idealism is misplaced. Sad to say, the primary motivating factor for the great majority of students is the grade. Graded quizzes work wonders in increasing class attendance." At the other end of the country, a freshman student at Slippery Rock University in Pennsylvania writes: "The majority of students know only one way of conducting themselves in a classroom setting, namely, do what you have to, and only then do it when it means a good grade." She then concludes with a plea for more "organization," that is, for more coercion.

It is clear that coercing freedom is an inherent contradiction. At the same time, the students' demand for structure reflects their sense that they have not yet developed the internal discipline that is indispensable for progress in learning. A seasoned professor of mathematics who recently returned to school to explore a fresh area of learning comments that as she was trying to master her new field she needed more structure and discipline at the beginning, because she was outside her field. She says that most of her life she had been self-taught, even that she had taught some subjects without much formal training. She was now seeking out a class that would force her to do things that ordinarily she would not do, be it writing, taking a test, or learning some of the boring but essential topics or skills. After many years of teaching, this professor seems now to question some of her earlier "creativity" and "self-taughtness," since she suggested that some basic facts and skills eluded her because she was unwilling to submit to the common discipline.

To some extent, resolution of the freedom-versus-discipline issue is subject to pendulum swings. In the 1960s, there was movement away from discipline, because many requirements were imposed, and instruction did not seem sufficiently concerned with eliciting the consent of those to be taught. We now face the consequences of freedom granted that has led to scatteredness and superficiality. However, how is one to balance freedom and discipline? Boling suggests two separate types of courses. Yet, it seems to me that every course has to perform a balancing act. Discipline without the student's consent is likely to lead to some easily forgotten learning. As one student has written (Becker and others, 1968, p. 60): "I've gone into classes where that's all you could do is memorize, memorize, and memorize. And, then you go in to take the final, and you put it all down on the paper, everything you've memorized, and then you forget it. You walk out of the class, and your mind is purged—perfectly clean. There is nothing in it. Someone asks you the next week what you learned in the class, and you couldn't tell them anything, because you didn't learn anything." Boling's exemplary teacher who taught him "freedom of expression" at the same time provided a very tight structure within which that freedom could be expressed. Boling's other revered teacher who insisted on discipline probably could rely on the affinity of interest with a student who years later would remember his course with so much enthusiasm. One wonders how other students who were not heading for a life of literary scholarship felt in his course. Might they have registered the confusion that Boling feels about some of his other teachers?

Teachers indeed walk a tightrope. They can lose students with too much structure, but they can also lose them with too much open-endedness. One needs to keep in mind that the undergraduate students quoted earlier were in the first two years of their college careers. One expects that they will be able and want to learn more on their own as they progress through college. Maturational progression will take place if instruction stimulates autonomy. Unfortunately, many seniors in many institutions still view learning as a set of responses to a body of knowledge that is imposed on them, not as a set of ideas in which they can become co-inquirers. In each course and during each class hour, teachers must therefore ask themselves how much structure their students need. At the same time, teachers must ask themselves what is the most that they can do in order to set their students free for their own explorations, for becoming aware of what they really want to know and what they must do to implement that desire. The magical link between freedom and discipline is motivation. Finding that link is a concrete task, which needs to be diligently worked for in every class hour. As Plato said long ago, enforced learning will not stay in the mind. Neither will half-empty freedom produce much beyond cognitive mush.

To reach our students, to encourage both freedom and discipline, and to find the motivational link require meticulous attention to students. It is obvious that the two teachers described by Boling were in many ways superb pedagogues for at least one student, but one wonders how much detailed day-to-day attention they gave to exploring the learning styles and learning stages of the students in their classes. For them, and for their colleagues everywhere, the instrument for encouraging better student learning is increased knowledge of students.

References

Becker, H. S., Geer, B., and Hughes, E. *Making the Grade: The Academic Side of College Life*. New York: Wiley, 1968.

Whitehead, A. N. *The Aims of Education*. New York: Macmillan, 1967. (Originally published 1929.)

Ronald Boling is a graduate student at the University of Florida who is beginning his doctoral course work in English.

The literature on new approaches to teaching college students is reviewed.

Additional Sources

A rich array of books is available to college instructors who seek to orient their teaching on a sophisticated understanding of their students. The following annotated list gives a sense of the variety of studies and includes some major contributions.

Astin, A. W. *Four Critical Years: Effects of College on Beliefs, Attitudes, and Knowledge.* San Francsico: Jossey-Bass, 1977.

Astin, A. W., and Panos, R. J. *The Educational and Vocational Development of College Students.* Washington, D.C.: American Council on Education, 1969.

Both books grow out of continuing studies of very large college student populations. They provide knowledge about effects of the academic and nonacademic environment on students' development and have suggestive implications for classroom teaching.

Axelrod, J. *The University Teacher as Artist.* San Francisco: Jossey-Bass, 1979.

This book, based on interviews and in-class observations, analyzes what makes classroom teaching effective and captures the unique artistic dimensions of teaching.

J. Katz (Ed.). *Teaching as Though Students Mattered.* New Directions for
Teaching and Learning, no. 21. San Francisco: Jossey-Bass, March 1985.

Chickering, A. W. *Education and Identity.* San Francisco: Jossey-Bass, 1969.

Chickering develops a complex theory of student development. One of the aims of the book is to encourage institutions and individual faculty to shape college programs, curricula, and teaching in light of what is known about student characteristics and aspirations.

DeCoster, D., and Mable, P. *Understanding Today's Students.* San Francisco: Jossey-Bass, 1981.

This book is based on interviews with students in twenty-eight different institutions across the country. It provides the reader with a description of student attitudes and behavior both in and out of the classroom.

Eble, K. *The Craft of Teaching.* San Francisco: Jossey-Bass, 1979.
Eble, K. *The Aims of College Teaching.* San Francisco: Jossey-Bass, 1983.

During a period of uncertainties about classroom pedagogy, role diffusion, and the future of college teaching, Eble's books provide both practical guidance and a compelling statement on the integrity of education focused on the intersection of learning, teaching, and discovering.

Ericksen, S. *Motivation for Learning.* Ann Arbor: University of Michigan Press, 1974.

The emphasis in this book is on motivating students through an understanding of learning, personality development, and group dynamics. It draws upon both theory and practical experience.

Erikson, E. *Identity and the Life Cycle.* New York: International Universities Press, 1959.

This is a magisterial work and includes Erikson's influential tracing of stages of development. It is a major resource for understanding the steps by which college students arrive at their present phase. The book combines the insights of clinical psychiatry, psychoanalysis, ethnography, and literature.

Feldman, K. A., and Newcomb, T. M. *The Impact of College on Students.* San Francisco: Jossey-Bass, 1969.

In this compendium of research on higher education and college students, the authors present and interpret findings from almost 1,500 published and unpublished reports.

Gamson, Z., and Associates. *Liberating Education.* San Francisco: Jossey-Bass, 1984.

Based on an analysis of fourteen programs in a wide variety of colleges and universities, the book focuses on undergraduate education that aims at developing students' critical awareness and their powers to use what they learn.

Gullette, M. M. (Ed.). *The Art and Craft of Teaching.* Cambridge, Mass.: Harvard-Danforth Center for Teaching and Learning, 1982.

This is a practical guide written particularly for the beginning teacher. It represents the student perspective chiefly in the closeness of the contributors (recent teaching assistants at Harvard) to the students they teach.

Huizinga, J. *Homo Ludens: A Study of the Play-Element in Culture.* Boston: Beacon Press, 1955.

This book is a classic on the subject of play in Western thought. Huizinga contends that man, despite his claim to be *homo sapiens,* is no less *homo ludens,* a creature given to play and, because of this element in the personality, given to interacting with the world as if it were a game or theater.

Katz, J., and Associates. *No Time for Youth: Growth and Constraint in College Students.* San Francisco: Jossey-Bass, 1968.

This book is based on a four-year study in which the same students were followed throughout their college careers. It provides a many-sided description of the intellectual and emotional development of students. One chapter provides detailed case histories of two students. The book ends with proposals for curricular planning and teaching based on knowledge of student development.

Kegan, R. *The Evolving Self: Problem and Process in Human Development.* Cambridge, Mass.: Harvard University Press, 1982.

Kegan proposes to integrate thought and emotion in human development; he draws upon both Kohlberg's and Perry's work.

Keirsey, D., and Bates, M. *Please Understand Me: Character and Temperament Types.* Del Mar, Calif.: Prometheus Nemesis Books, 1978.

This is a general introduction to the Myers-Briggs Type Inventory

growing out of Jungian psychology. It is also a telling plea for epistemological pluralism, ways of learning found outside our respective
disciplines.

Kuhn, T. *The Structure of Scientific Revolutions*. Chicago: University of
Chicago Press, 1962.

This book provides an excellent stimulus for breaking into uncritical
habits of thought about the boundaries of knowledge. By understanding
the social and historical reasons for various ways of viewing the world,
teachers can use that knowledge to generate fresh thinking in themselves
and their students.

Loevinger, J. *Ego Development: Conception and Theories*. San Francisco:
Jossey-Bass, 1976.

Loevinger offers a rich theoretical basis for a fuller understanding of
student development as it affects student learning and as it can affect a
teacher's teaching.

Lowman, J. *Mastering the Techniques of Teaching*. San Francisco: Jossey-
Bass, 1984.

A thorough and practical guide to all aspects of college teaching, this
book advocates teaching that promotes student involvement and independence.

McKeachie, W. J. *Teaching Tips*. Lexington, Mass.: Heath, 1969.

This is a practical guidebook by one of the leading researchers on college teaching. It covers classroom discussions, lectures, papers, exams,
the project method and many other topics.

Mann, R. D., and others. *The College Classroom*. New York: Wiley, 1970.

This book provides detailed descriptions of the variety of student types
one encounters in the classroom. It sharpens one's sense of the difficulty
of responding to so many different personalities and styles all at once.

Murphy, L., and Ladd, H. *Emotional Factors in Learning*. New York:
Columbia University Press, 1944.

This is a pioneering work out of Sarah Lawrence College that focuses on
the emotional aspects of learning, highly relevant to students but often
bypassed by professors.

Perry, W. G., Jr. *Forms of Intellectual and Ethical Development in the College Years*. New York: Holt, Rinehart and Winston, 1970.

In this path-breaking book Perry charts, on the basis of extensive interviews with college students, three major stages (absolute, relative, and commitment) through which the student passes as he or she encounters the new experience of university life.

Sanford, N., and others. *The American College*. Wiley, 1962.

This book exerted a major influence on studies of college students, the curriculum, and the behavior and organization of institutions. It includes a special section on professors and teaching.

White, R. W. *Lives in Progress*. Holt, Rinehart and Winston, 1975.

White provides a theoretical framework and focuses on the case histories of three students who are presented in their evolution before, during, and after college. It provides dimensions of students' lives that often are not very visible in the classroom.

Whiteley, J. M., and Associates. *Character Development in College Students*. Vol. 1. Schenectady, N.Y.: Character Research Press, 1982.

This is a report of the Sierra project at the University of California, Irvine, in which a program is designed to encompass the entire social milieu as well as the formal courses of study of a diverse group of students.

Wilson, R. C., Gaff, J. G., Dienst, E. R., Wood, L., and Bavry, J. L. *College Professors and Their Impacts on Students*. New York: Wiley, 1975.

This book draws upon data from 1,000 faculty members at six colleges and universities to identify faculty attitudes, values, activities, and teaching practices. From this basis and additional information from students, the authors analyze the impact teachers have on students and offer suggestions about how faculty members might increase their impact.

Index